LUKE JERRAM
ART, SCIENCE & PLAY

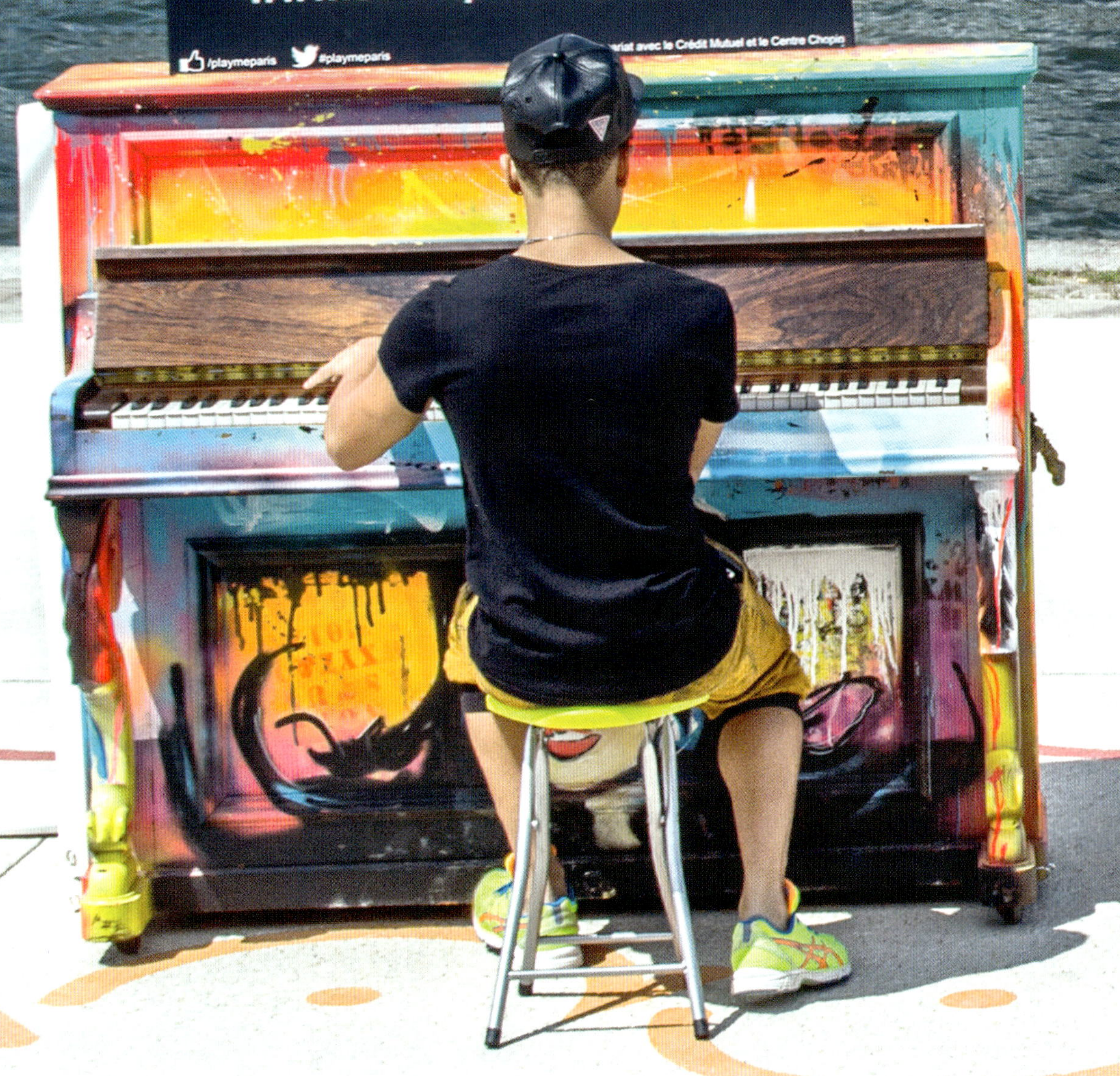

Play Me, I'm Yours
www.streetpianosparis.com
/playmeparis
#playmeparis

LUKE JERRAM
ART, SCIENCE & PLAY

edited by Gemma Brace and Leela Thornfield

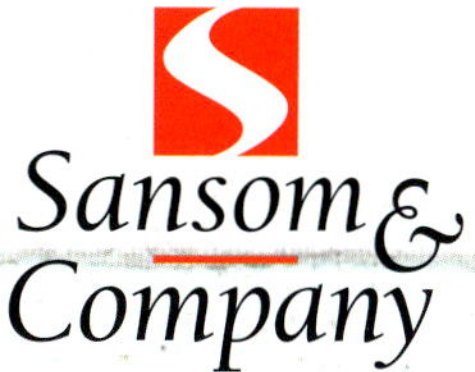

Thanks to my ever-supportive parents,
my wonderful wife Shelina and our
inspirational children Maya and Nico.

First published in 2019 by Sansom and Company,
a publishing imprint of Redcliffe Press Ltd.,
81ɢ Pembroke Road, Bristol BS8 3EA
www.sansomandcompany.co.uk | info@sansomandcompany.co.uk

ISBN 978-1-911408-48-2

British Library Cataloguing-in-Publication Data
A catalogue record for this book is available from the British Library.

Design and typesetting by E&P Design, Bath

Printed and bound by Zenith Media, Pontypool.
Sansom & Co is committed to being an environmentally-friendly publisher.
All our books are printed on sustainably-sourced paper.

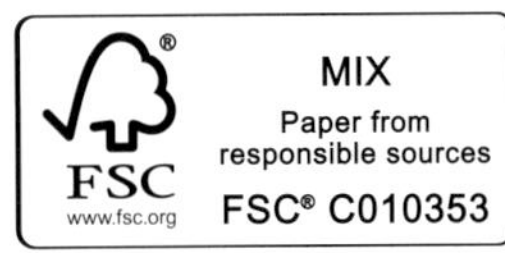

Front cover: *Museum of the Moon*, Liverpool Cathedral, 2018
Frontispiece: *Play Me, I'm Yours*, Paris, 2014

This publication was made possible with kind support from:

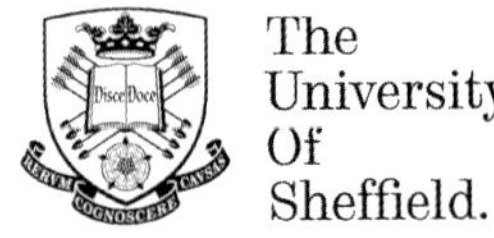

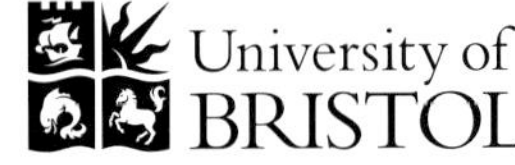

Contents

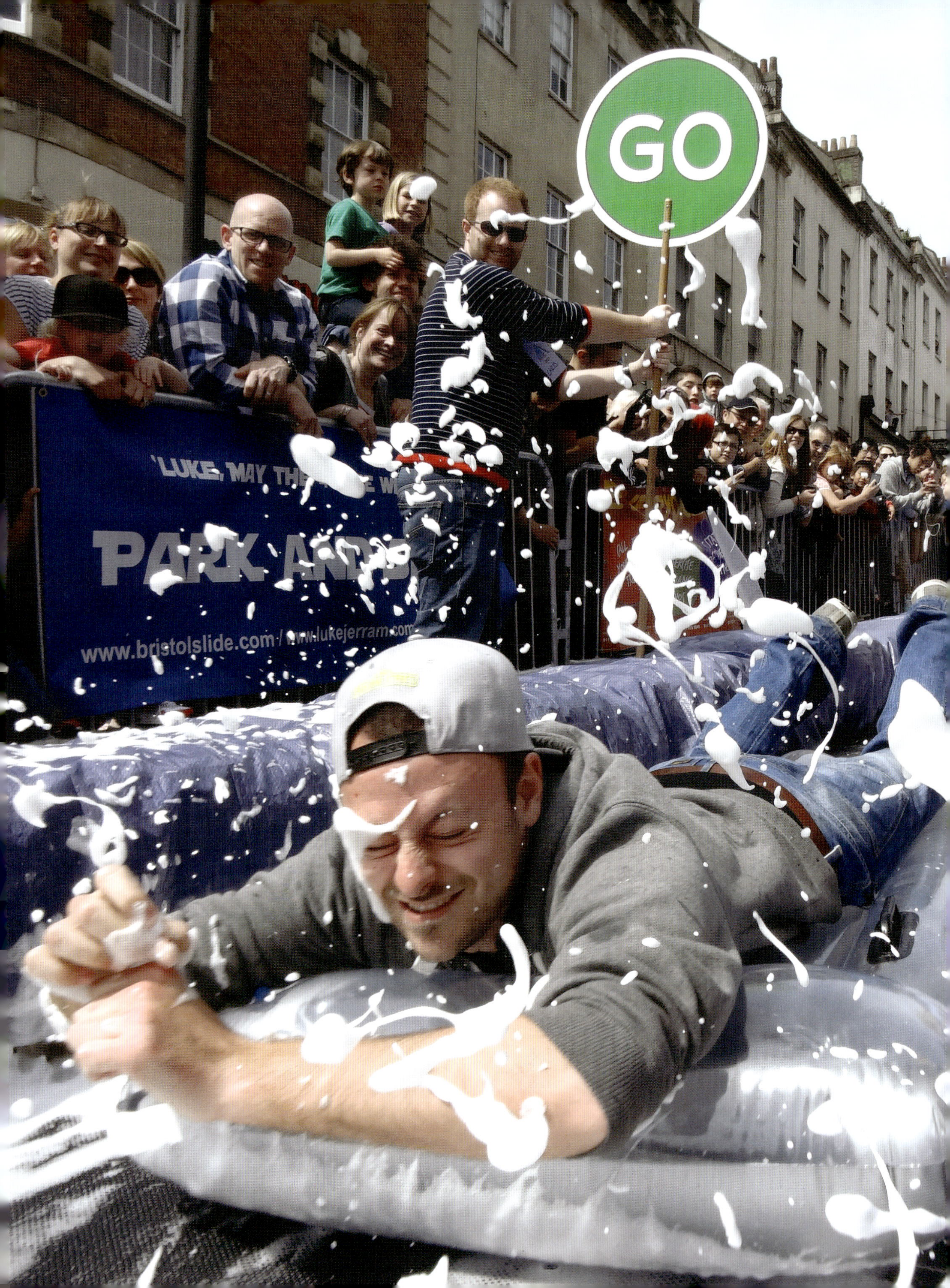

GO
'LUKE, MAY THE ... BE W...
PARK AND ...
www.bristolslide.com / www.lukejerram.com

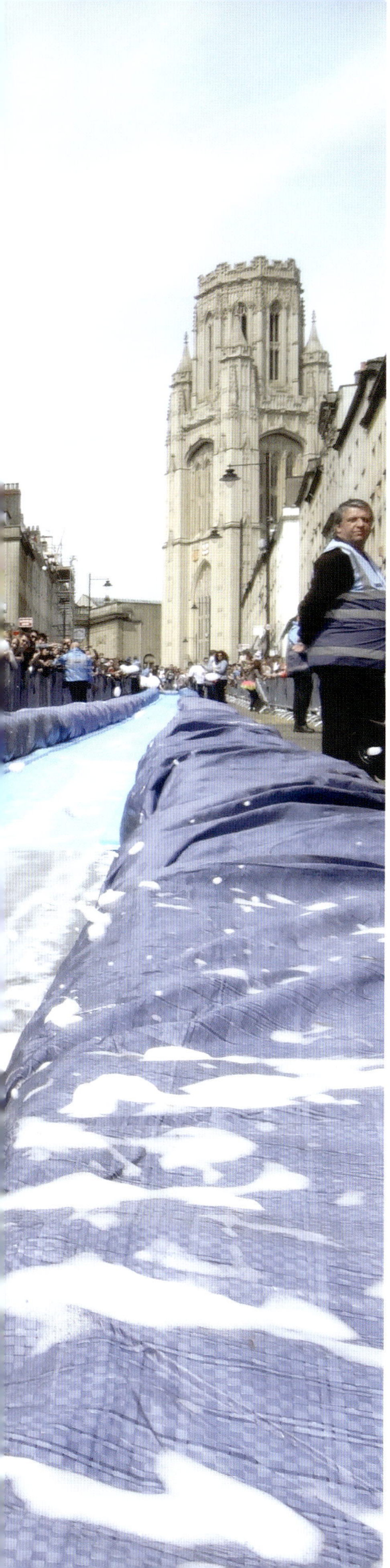

Foreword I

The first time I worked with Luke he flew *Sky Orchestra* over central Birmingham, transforming a leaden dawn sky with an enchanting artwork experienced by thousands of Brummies in their houses and the streets below. And as I watched people rush out of their homes, some only wrapped in towels and in dressing gowns, to gaze in wonder at the sights and sounds above, I witnessed what I've come to cherish time and time again through Luke's artworks, like *Park and Slide* (left) and *Withdrawn*. That through the power of his extraordinary imagination he has a rare gift for making work that creates communities. I saw it again on the very first day of his now global sensation *Play Me, I'm Yours* in Birmingham, 2007, when a black teenager approached a piano and played a flawless Beethoven piano sonata, stunning his school mates and drawing crowds of local people to him to enjoy his secret gift. Luke is an artist for our times. In an increasingly divided and atomised world his works become a gathering space, drawing people together through joyful and evocative shared experiences.

Defying the usual labels of the art world, Luke is variously described as an inventor, engineer, activist, educator and entrepreneur. I'd add magician to that list too, for once you've experienced his work, our city streets, railway stations and forests are never perceived in quite the same way again. Because in transforming the possibilities of what can happen in public space; in making the everyday feel both magical and impossible, he burns images and experiences into our own individual and collective imaginations that last forever.

A recent TV documentary about Luke's work begins with the words 'Luke Jerram is probably the most famous artist you've never heard of'. Many artists would smart at that description, but not Luke. A modest, deeply generous and brilliant artist, with a seemingly infinite ability to generate extraordinary ideas and experiences, Luke's artworks are a gift, reminding us of the common bonds that hold us together.

Mark Ball
Creative Director, Manchester International Festival

Park and Slide | *Bristol, 2014*

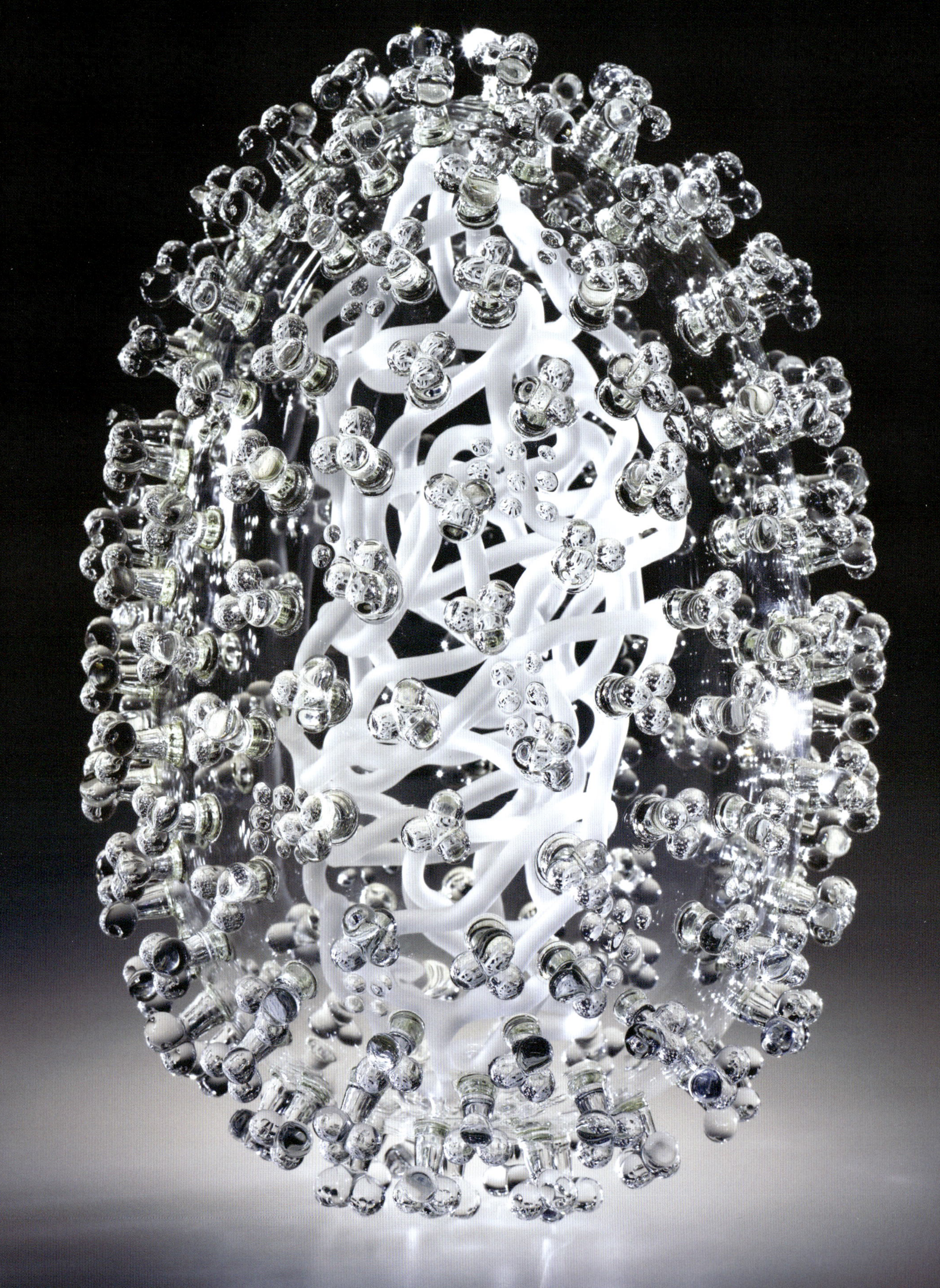

Foreword II

The first time I met him, Luke was carrying a box. Inside was a stunning glass bug: a sculpture of the AIDS virus. I thought Wellcome Collection should acquire it. Luke wondered if the cost of making it plus travel expenses, seemed reasonable; I encouraged him to come back with a price that included a more generous margin for himself.

Millions of times larger than its subject matter, the work's un-show-offy surface and accurate form gave transparent access to an intriguing and literally sickening tension at its core: a biological entity that appears beautiful, but that is also deadly dangerous and attractively fatal. Like a number of Luke's works, *Glass Microbiology* (left) is partly about scale; in this case, putting the invisibly small into the palms of our hands.

An old-fashioned idea that infuses Luke's oeuvre is curiosity. Distinct from its more passive cousin wonder, this is the instinct to prod and push the world in order to reveal a secret or two, while nevertheless resisting the temptation to explode its beguiling mysteries. Luke's work materialises a blue-skied, open-eyed and open-minded eagerness to find things out, but is also flavoured with an uncanny ability to unknow some of our knowns, encouraging us to pause and re-examine things with which we have become familiar.

Another adjective springs to mind: generous. *Museum of the Moon* is a touring exhibition; but far from simply moving an inflatable sculpture from one venue to the next, the project makes as much as it can of the places it lands, gathering personal stories and myths as it does – a kind of wandering lunar muse with a deep respect for local differences. His practice often leaves space for other artists, performers, scientists, anthropologists, and indeed the rest of us, to explore our own dreams, fears and perspectives. The gap between seeing and feeling in his work can be as thin as a piece of glass, but he still manages to lodge enough potential energy there to ensure that extraordinary and emergent properties can flourish.

Thanks Luke.

Ken Arnold
Creative Director, Wellcome Trust
Director, Medical Museion, Copenhagen University

Glass Microbiology: Swine Flu | 2009

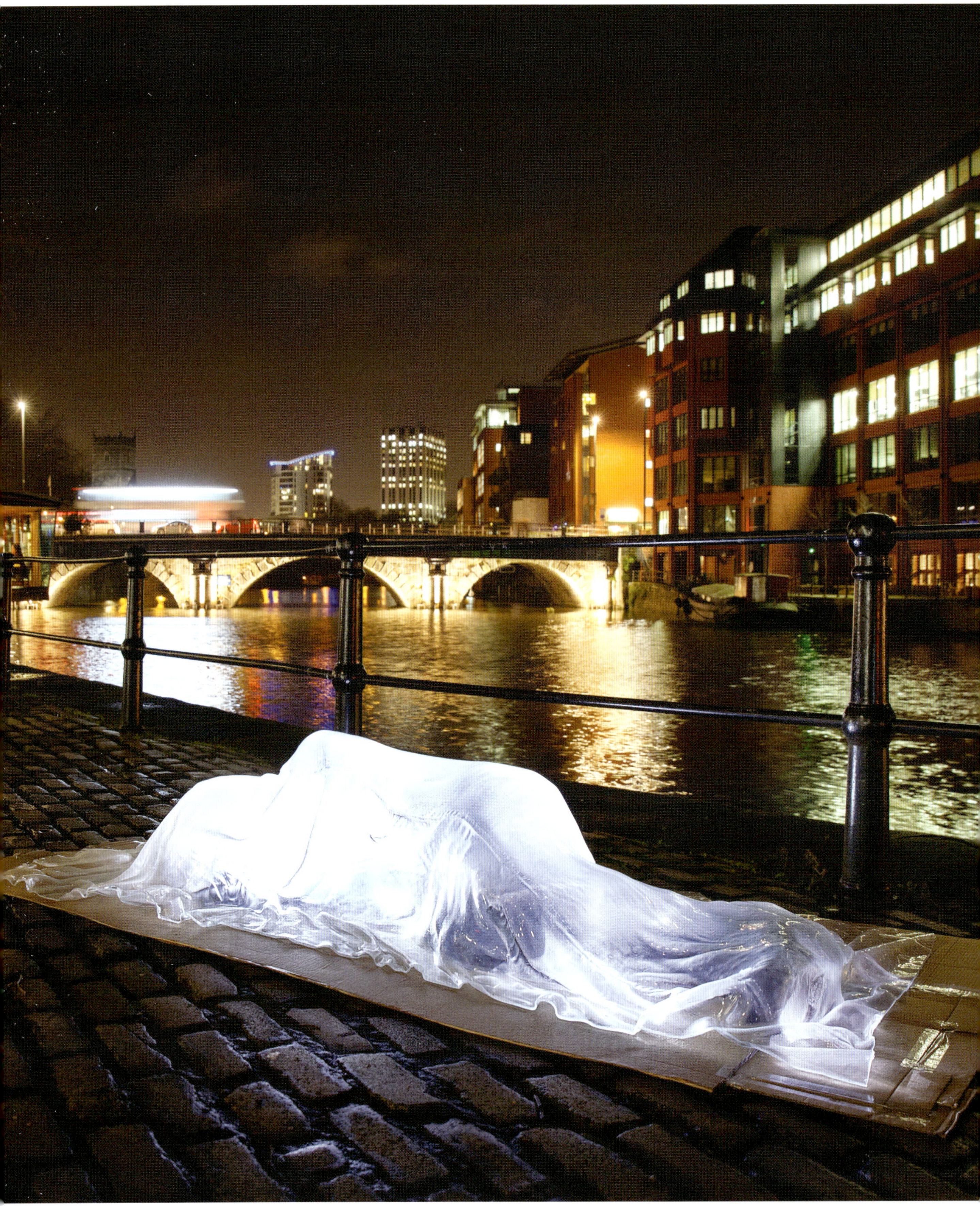

Introduction

I've devoted the past 21 years as an artist to creating unique and hopefully memorable experiences and objects for people to interrogate and enjoy. It's not entirely selfless as each artwork is also something I've wanted to personally experience. They are often experimental, providing me with multiple opportunities such as learning the invisible rules of public interaction, exploring the phenomenon of perception, experimenting with design and technology, and even having fun. Communicating with audiences on many different levels, I try to make artworks which have multiple doors of entry so they can be accessed and enjoyed by all; from adults to children, from the UK or abroad, and from fellow artists, to scientists, engineers, musicians and school students.

On the surface my artworks can seem disconnected but there are actually many narratives that draw them together. Learning from each artwork and then moving on, I'm continually re-inventing my practice whilst maintaining key areas of interest and enquiry. I like to think that this approach has meant I've been able to adapt to new opportunities and that I'll still be surprised by the artwork I make in five years' time. However, this does perhaps come at a cost, in that for many years it's been hard for people seeing my work to say 'that looks like an artwork by Luke Jerram'. This book is a way of bringing together all of these seemingly disparate projects and presenting them as an interconnected body of work.

There are multiple ways to categorise my artworks and numerous different connections and threads to follow between them. Just one of the connecting themes, which I feel is important to consider, is scale; how we perceive objects that are too large or too small for our senses. I'm interested in exploring what happens to an object if it is scaled-up or shrunk down; or made on a scale comparable to the viewer's own body. Then, there is the investigation of sound and vibration, a more specific part of my perceptual research that has led to a number of works such as *Tide, Aeolus, Plant Orchestra* and *Harrison's Garden*. I am also interested in the ways that sound and music have the potential to paint pictures in our imagination, transforming the act of listening into a visual experience. This phenomenon is one of the inspirations behind *Sky Orchestra*, whereas other works, such as *Tōhoku Japanese Earthquake* and *Apollo,* are connected by both solidifying sound, and making invisible sound waves visible. ▶

Invisible Homeless | *Bristol, 2015*

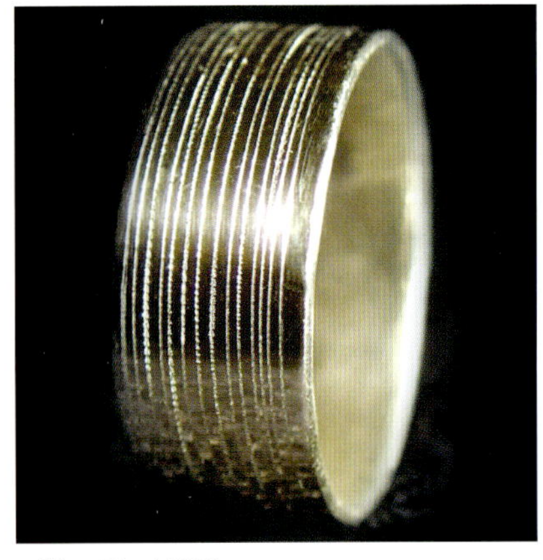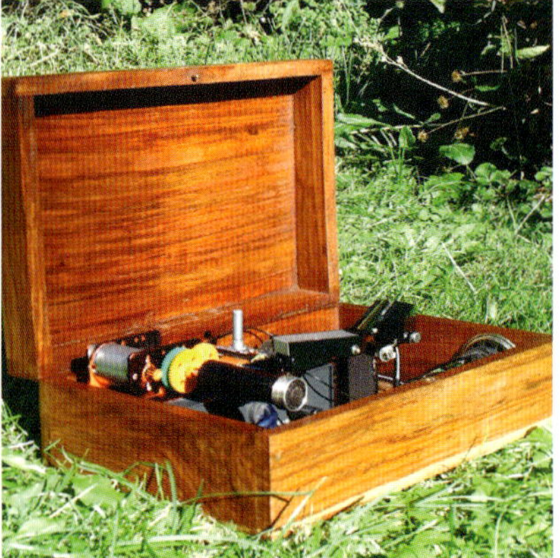

Talking Ring | 2007

Other recurrent themes are those of participation and play (allowing space for others' creativity), which can be seen in projects such as *Play Me, I'm Yours, Park and Slide* and *Lullaby*. These artworks only become complete with the animation of the public. As with *1000 Flowers*, they are also quite generous, almost like a gift to the community. I have even made personalised 'gift' artworks such as *Wellcome Portrait* and *Talking Ring*.

However, after some debate and a degree of personal conflict, I have settled on the broad titles of *People, Perception* and *Place,* under which a selection of my key projects are to be considered. These ideas are by no means exhaustive – many of the featured projects could sit equally well within each of these chapters – but they do offer an open, thematic way to navigate my practice.

Retinal Memory Volume was my very first project which blended art and science and was developed while I was still at art college. I had applied to be part of the *European Media Art Festival* in Germany, and to my surprise I was accepted. It was an amazing experience to be flown over to Osnabrück and put-up in a local hotel to install the artwork. They paid me a grand fee of €100, which I promptly lost as it fell out of my back pocket on the way home. I was young and naïve at the time, but this pivotal experience kick-started my career of touring artworks as I was consequentially invited to show this same work at Wolfsburg Castle in Germany, *Encounters* in Paris, and in Lisbon for *Cyber '98*.

As an artist I feel that it's important to embrace and accept risk and even failure. The artworks I make are concept-driven and often involve innovative technology or trying something new that is just slightly out of my comfort zone. While also keeping my life interesting, it means that new artworks are in effect prototypes and things don't always go exactly to plan. In retrospect, thinking back to older artworks, the idea of fusing water with electricity and moving parts for *Tide* in 2001 was asking for trouble.

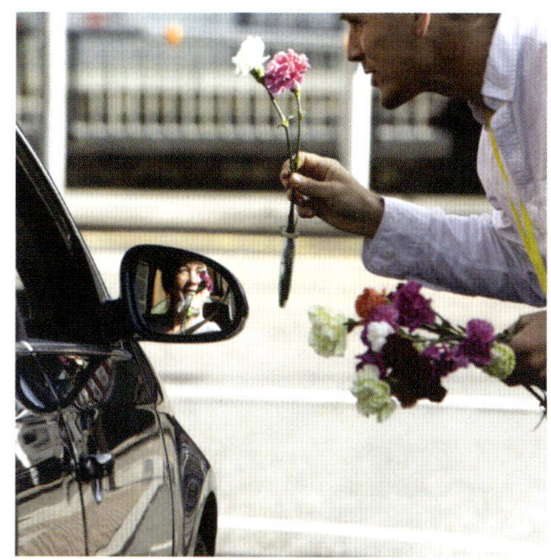

1000 Flowers | *Cork Midsummer Festival, 2018*

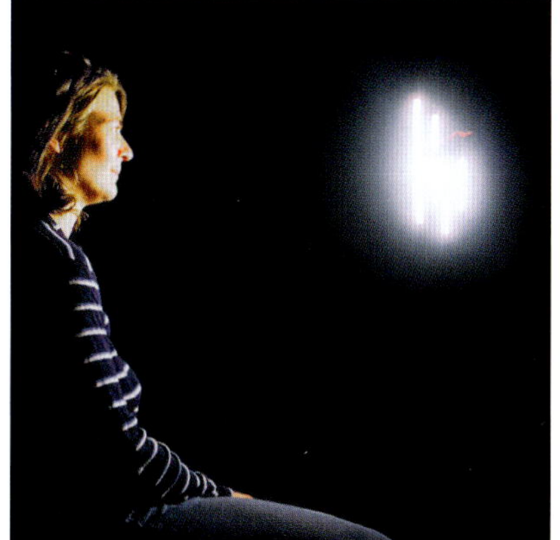

Retinal Memory Volume | *1997*

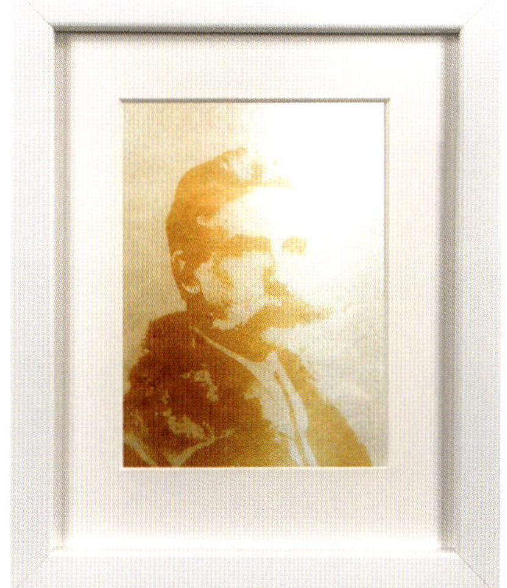

Wellcome Portrait | *2004*

A little while later in 2008, I'd been invited to present *Sky Orchestra* over Birmingham, with members of the Birmingham Symphony Orchestra performing in the hot air balloons. We all turned up at 6am but it was far too windy to fly. However, the musicians were on music union rates so they all had to be paid, plus we had to pay all the pilots for turning up even though they couldn't launch the balloons. I'd promised Birmingham City Council to reach 100,000 people across the city with a large-scale artwork, but effectively had already blown half of the budget before I'd started. I had to come up with another idea quickly for half of the original budget and that's when the idea for *Play Me, I'm Yours* was born. This project has triggered a global movement of pianos installed in public places for people to play, and the concept has become part of everyday urban culture.

There are often unexpected outcomes that reveal themselves after the creation of each artwork and it feels important to allow room for them. For example, *Play Me, I'm Yours,* has led to several marriages with strangers meeting over a piano for the first time and falling in love. Performers have been 'discovered' and given recording contracts, and the artwork has even helped to lead to a change in UK music licensing laws after it was discussed in the House of Lords; you no longer need a license to install a street piano in the UK.

We can all come up with ideas in the pub on a Friday night. The trick is being able to take those ideas and make them happen. Collaboration is key to the success of my practice and it is only with specialist teams of glassblowers, composers, engineers and even balloon manufacturers that I'm able to realise most of my artworks. I get excited about opening-up new conversations with organisations and finding ways to enable artworks to come into being. It's through these collaborations that anything becomes possible. Interestingly, on the day before the inaugural presentation of *Play Me, I'm Yours* was due to launch in Birmingham, my appendix burst and I was in hospital for a week or so. While there, a doctor came to me with the *Guardian* newspaper and asked 'how have you managed to install 15 pianos across the city when you've been here in bed for the past three days?'. I had to explain that as with most of my artworks it was very much a team effort.

After 21 years of practice I feel like I've only just learnt how to be an artist and can now spread my wings and get a sense of what I might be making in the future. I can't wait to see what sort of artworks will come into being next!

Luke Jerram

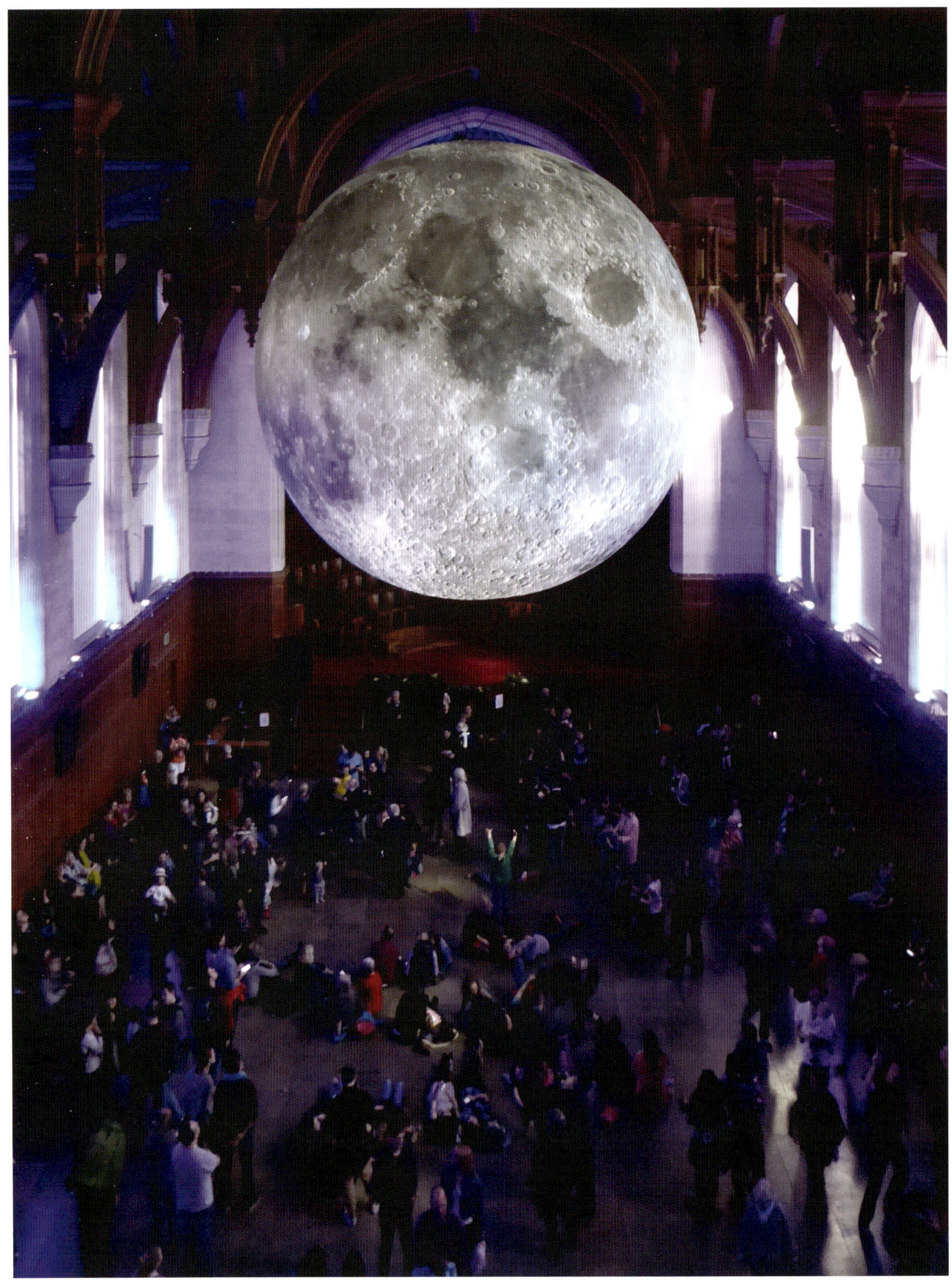

Museum of the Moon | *University of Bristol, 2017*

People

I remember watching performance art when I was at college and thinking that it was the performer on stage that was having the most interesting time. Perhaps, as a response to this, for some of my artworks I have consciously placed other people at the heart of the experience. Artworks, such as *Play Me, I'm Yours,* act as blank canvases through which the public can explore their own creativity. The street pianos turn amateur musicians who might not normally have the confidence to play to an audience into street performers. These people become the centre of the artwork.

Park and Slide only really comes into existence when activated by the public. It was animated by both the presence of people sliding down it and the crowds of people watching. Without people it's just a sheet of plastic and some hay bales. It came as a surprise to see many of the sliders dressed up; there was a gorilla, a few supermen, even a banana. These costumes added theatricality and a sense of fun, but also provided a useful degree of anonymity at such a high profile event. While functioning as installation artworks in their own right, *Museum of the Moon* and *Withdrawn* also act as a venue or a stage providing a space for others to perform.

In our digital age, everyone can be seen as a creative agent. With the proliferation of smart phones and social media, people have the capacity to become their own broadcasting channel. The success of *Play Me, I'm Yours* and *Museum of the Moon* is in part due to the opportunity they allow for the public to both express themselves and share their experience online. To date, 17,000 #MuseumoftheMoon images have been posted on Instagram.

We have a responsibility to consider how our cities and towns can be navigated and animated by the people that live in them for present and future generations. For the duration of time that we each live in a city we have a stake in its wellbeing, and it's up to us to define its character. *Park and Slide* enabled people to think about their urban environment in a new and playful way, and, by removing all the traffic from the road, take ownership of it. It was even financed through crowdfunding from local residents, which strengthened this sense of ownership.

Play Me, I'm Yours, Sky Orchestra and *Lullaby* question the notion of public versus private space. Broadcasting music into people's houses at potentially anti-social times of the day can be considered a form of audio graffiti. Rather than taking place in the centre of town or in a museum, these artworks are designed to deliver an experience directly to people's homes and peripheral communities.

Sky Orchestra

2003–2013 | skyorchestra.co.uk

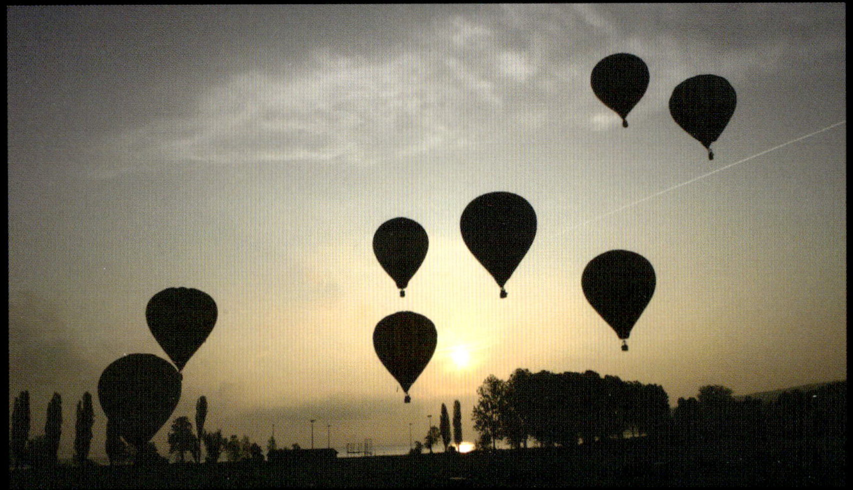

Yverdon, Switzerland, 2005

Sky Orchestra is a live artwork designed to deliver music to sleeping people from the sky. Comprising seven hot air balloons, each with speakers attached, the *Sky Orchestra* takes off at dawn and flies across a city with each balloon playing a different element of a musical score. Creating a massive audio landscape, many thousands of people experience the *Sky Orchestra* as the balloons fly over their homes. Through delivering a surround-sound experience to people on the edge of sleep, Luke aims to acoustically seed their imaginations.

The airborne project is both a vast spectacular performance as well as an intimate, personal experience. A form of acoustic urban art, *Sky Orchestra* questions the boundaries of public artwork, private space and the ownership of the sky.

Sky Orchestra was a collaboration between Luke, award-winning composer Dan Jones, and lead pilot Peter Dalby. During the development of the artwork Luke worked with sleep psychologists at University of West of England, Bristol, to investigate the effects of sound on sleep. Since the first *Sky Orchestra* performance in Bristol in 2003, it has also launched *Sydney Festival*, Australia; performed for the Royal Shakespeare Company over Stratford-upon-Avon, and been presented in London for the 2012 Olympics.

LJ: *I first had the idea for **Sky Orchestra** when I experienced the call to prayer at 3am in Tunisia. The voices calling from many different areas of the town simultaneously opened up a kind of sculptural map in my imagination. It was a beautiful experience, which lifted me in to a space on the edge of sleep. I could see the layers of sound building onto one another. It was the first artwork I made which delivered a creative experience directly to people in their own communities.*

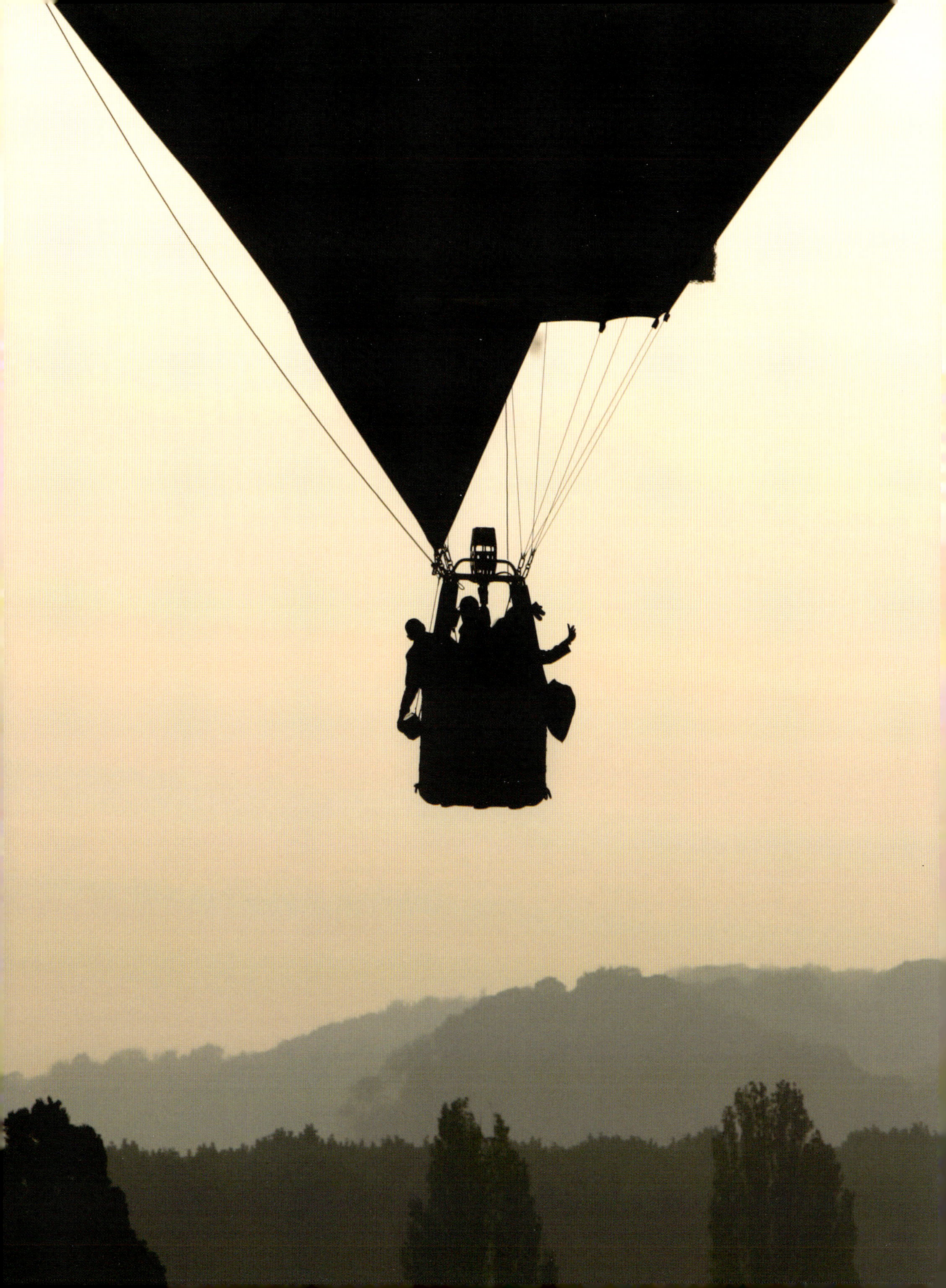

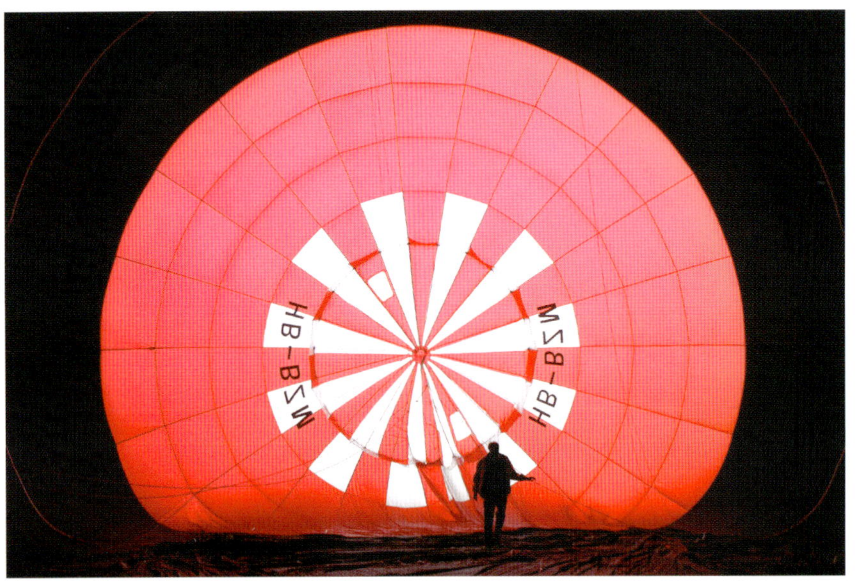

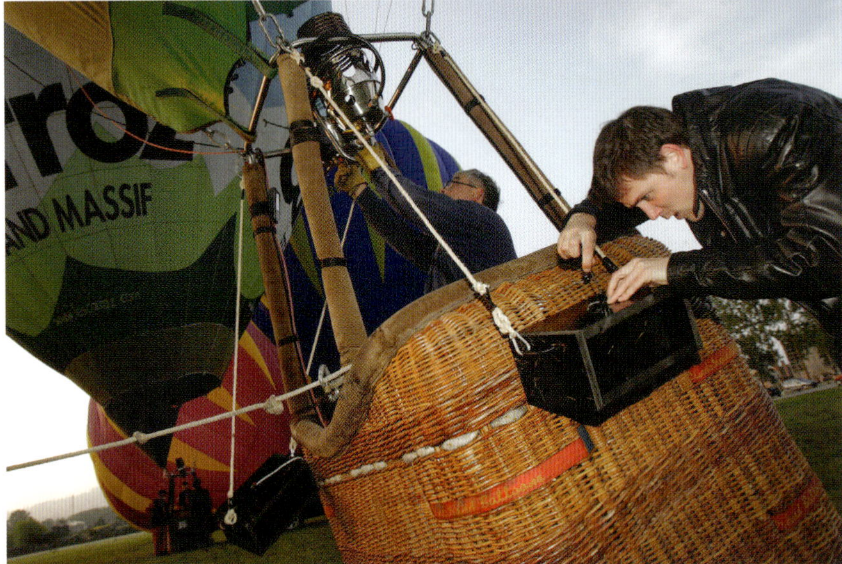

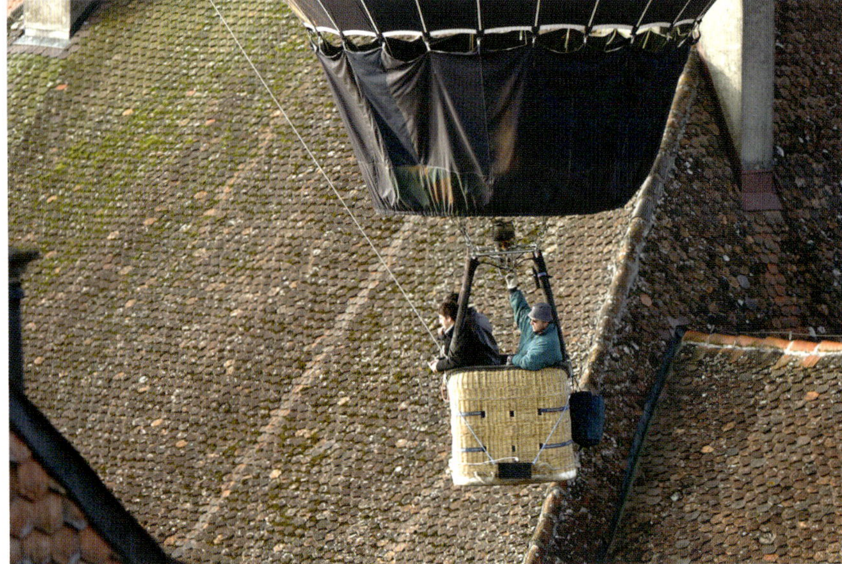

Yverdon, Switzerland, 2005

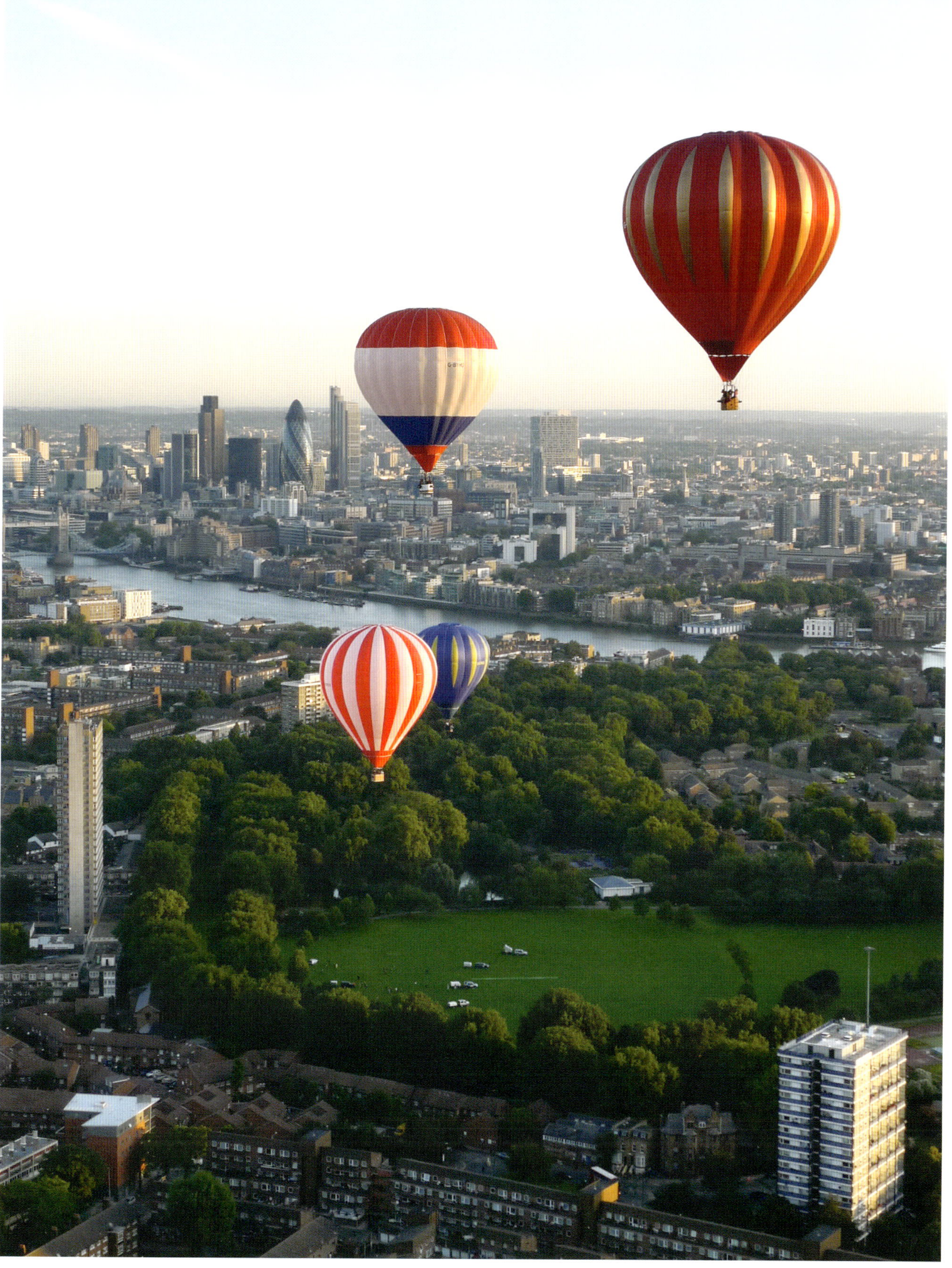

London, 2011

Play Me, I'm Yours

2008–2019 | streetpianos.com

First commissioned in Birmingham in 2008, 15 pianos were installed across the city for three weeks for people to play. Since then, *Play Me, I'm Yours* has toured to 60 cities across the globe, from Tokyo to New York, with more than 1,900 street pianos installed in total.

Located on streets, in public parks, markets and train stations, the pianos are available for everyone to play and enjoy. *Play Me, I'm Yours* invites the public to engage with, activate, and take ownership of their urban environment, and to share their love of music and art. Decorated by local artists and community groups, the street pianos disrupt people's negotiation of their city and create a place for creative exchange.

Play Me, I'm Yours has enticed many hidden musicians out of the woodwork, and in countries where the instrument is rare and more valued it has provided opportunities for thousands of pianists who wouldn't normally have regular access. It has even attracted more famous musicians, such as John Legend, Elton John and Jamie Cullum, who have used the street pianos to reach their fans on a more informal public stage.

Many wonderful, uplifting and bizarre stories have come about from the project.

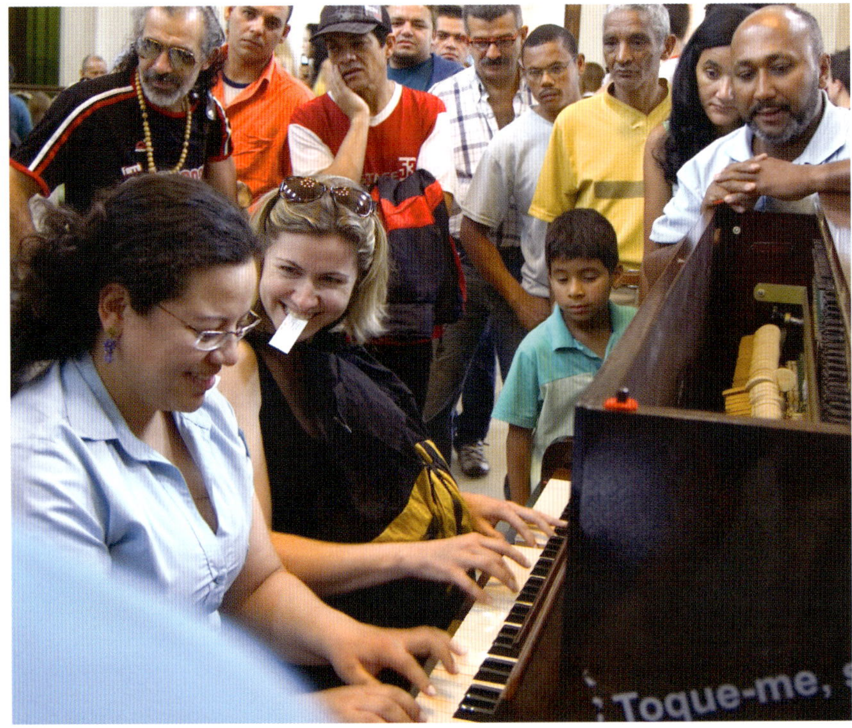

São Paulo, 2008

LJ: **The idea for Play Me, I'm Yours *came from visiting my local launderette. I saw the same people there each weekend and yet no one talked to one another. I realised that there must be hundreds of these invisible communities, regularly spending time with one another in silence. Placing a piano into the space was my solution to this problem; to act as a catalyst for conversation.***

▶ Bristol, 2009   ▶▶ New York, 2010

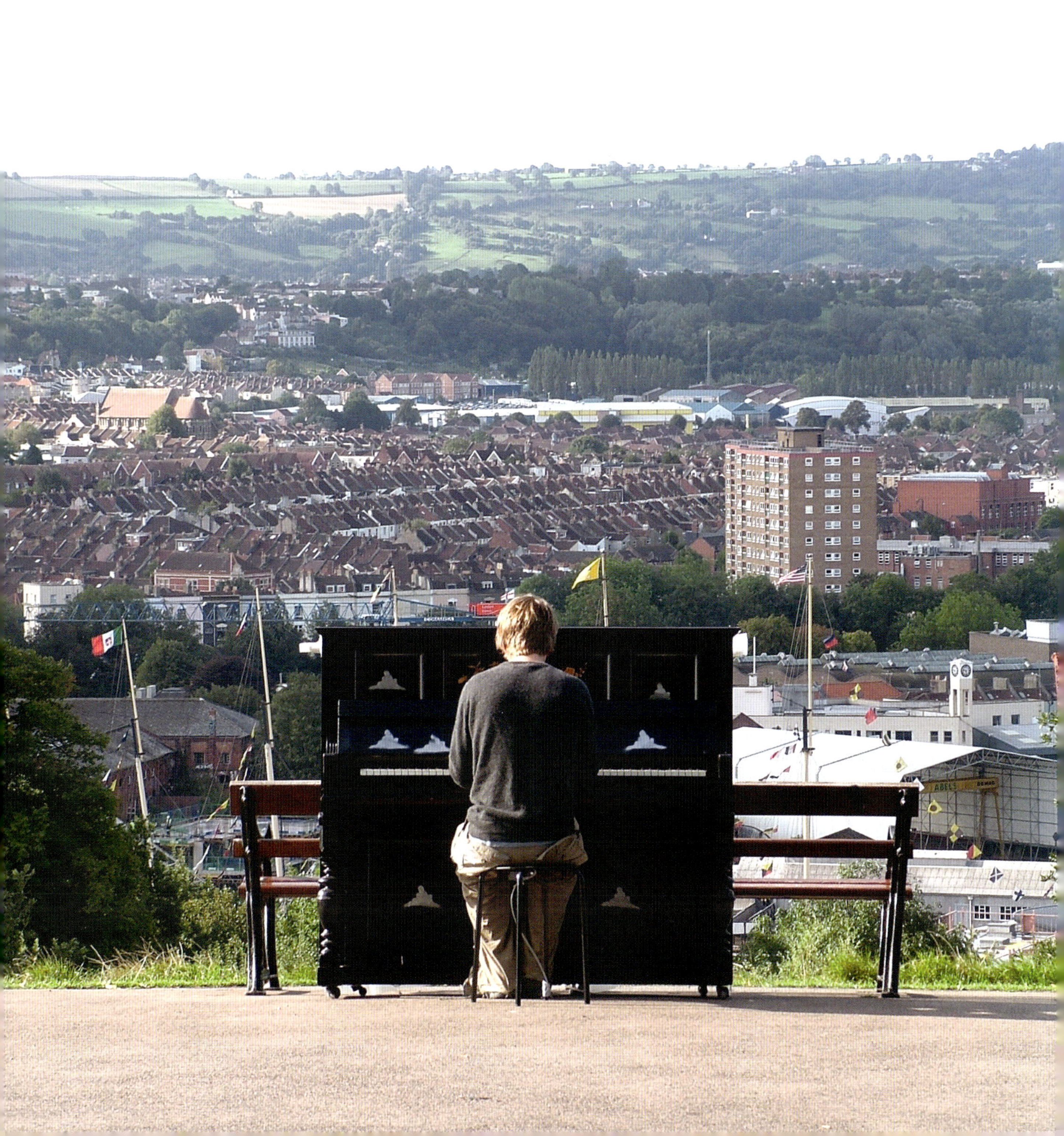

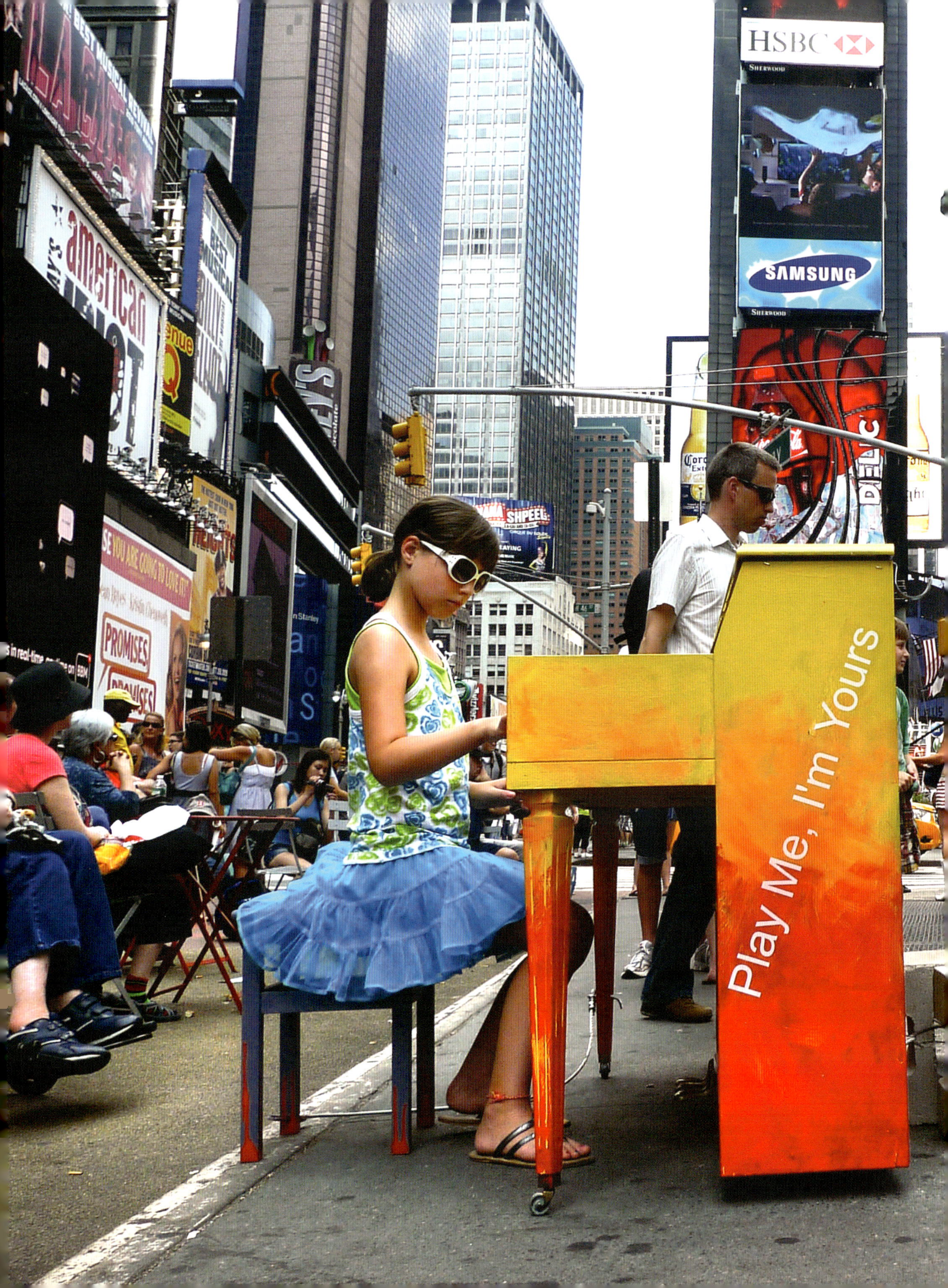

HSBC
SHERWOOD
SAMSUNG
SHERWOOD
american
PROMISES
PROMISES
Play Me, I'm Yours

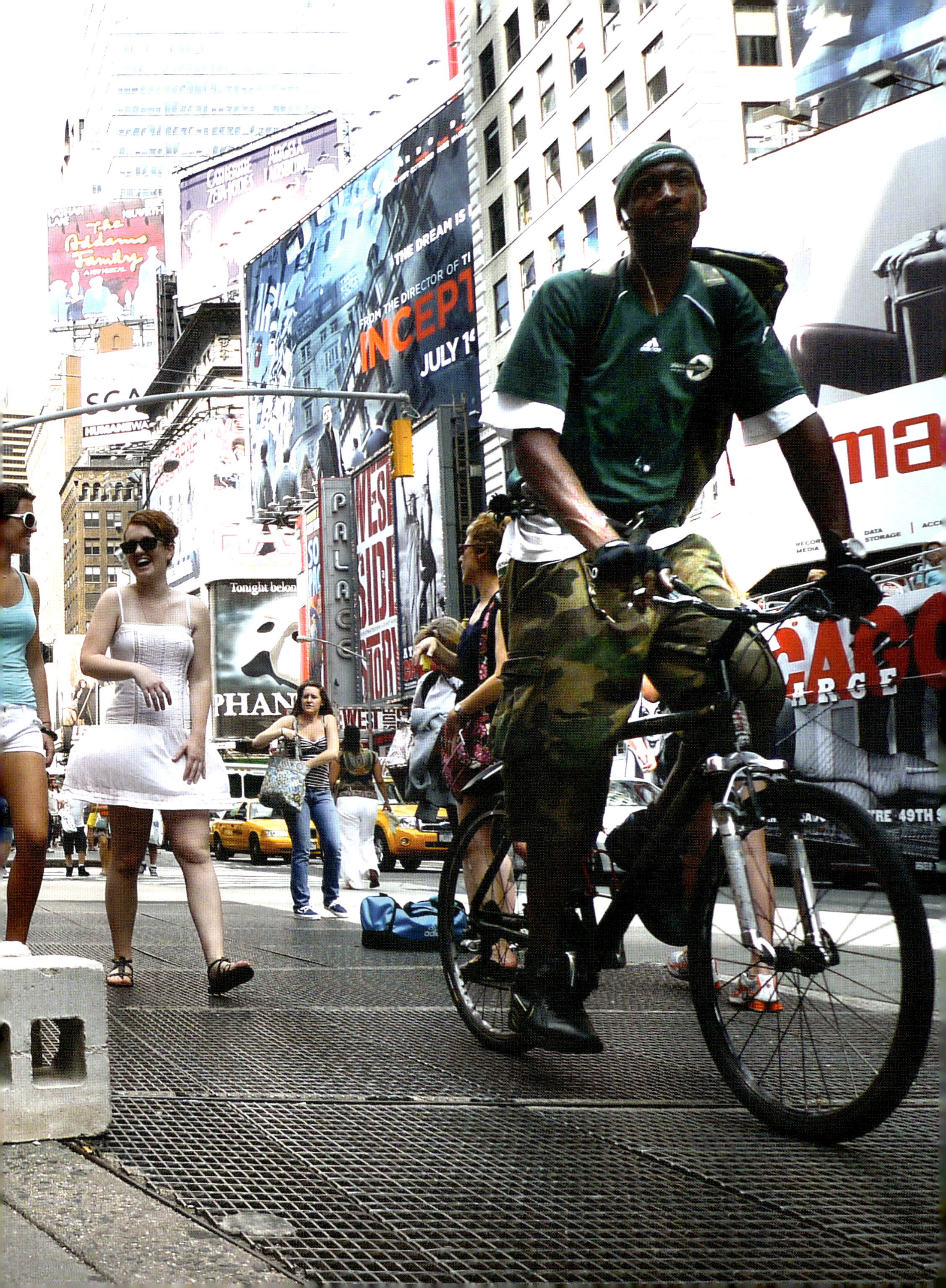

The Addams Family
A NEW MUSICAL
THE DREAM IS
FROM THE DIRECTOR OF T
INCEPT
JULY 1
SCA
WEST SIDE STORY
PALACE
Tonight belon
PHAN
ma
CAGO
RGE
TRE 49TH
RECORD
MEDIA
DATA
STORAGE
ACC

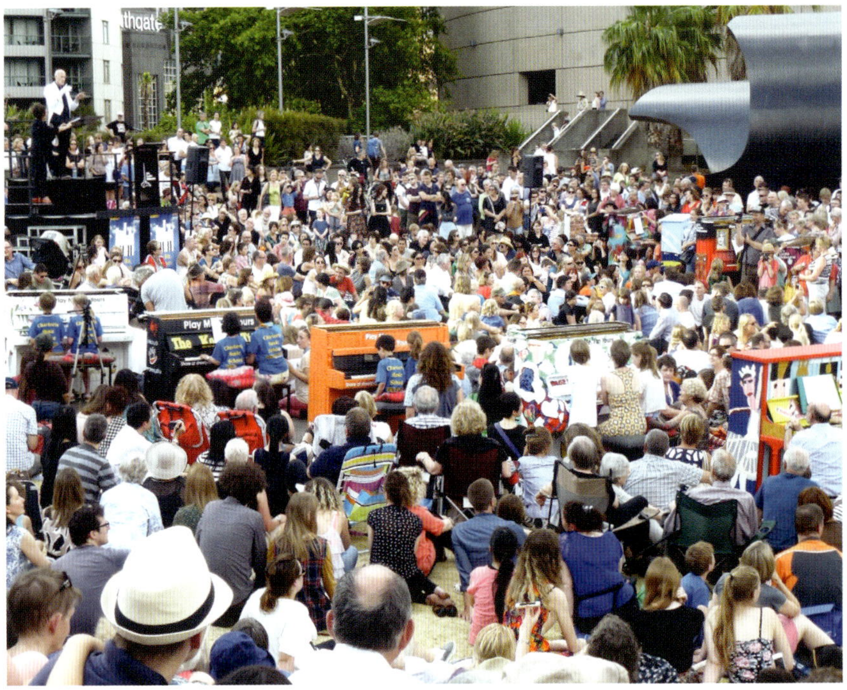

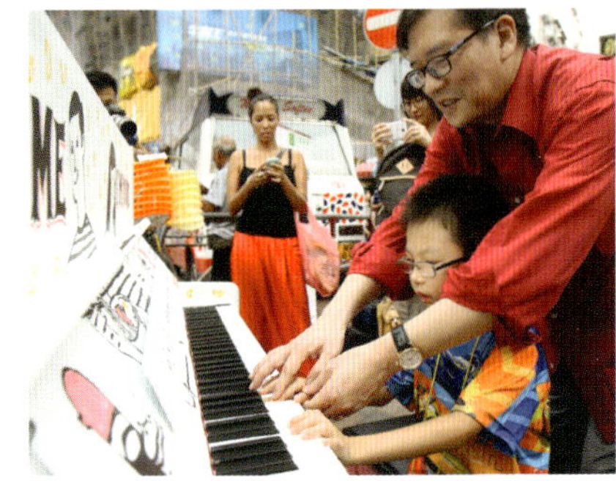

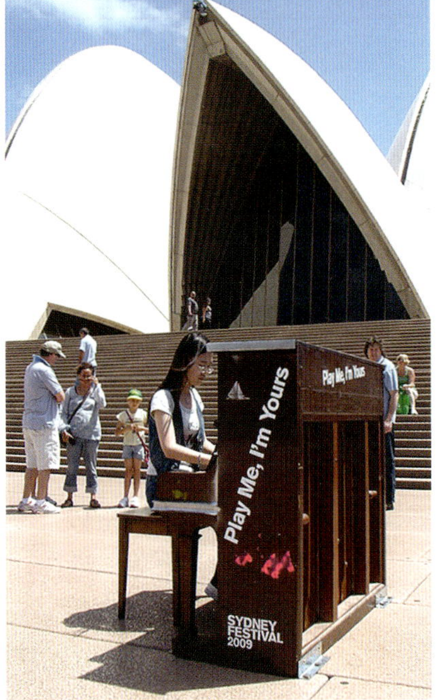

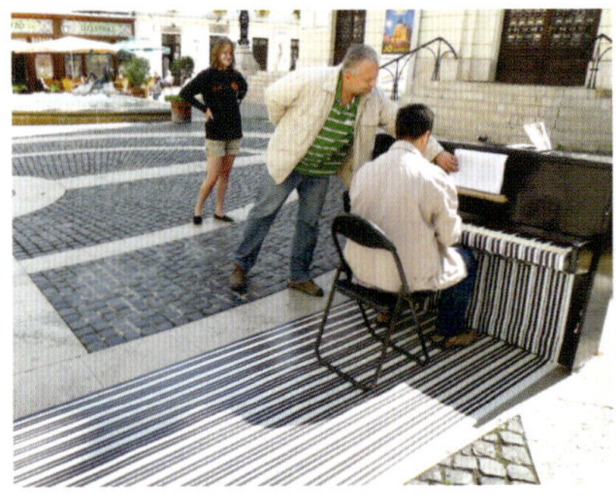

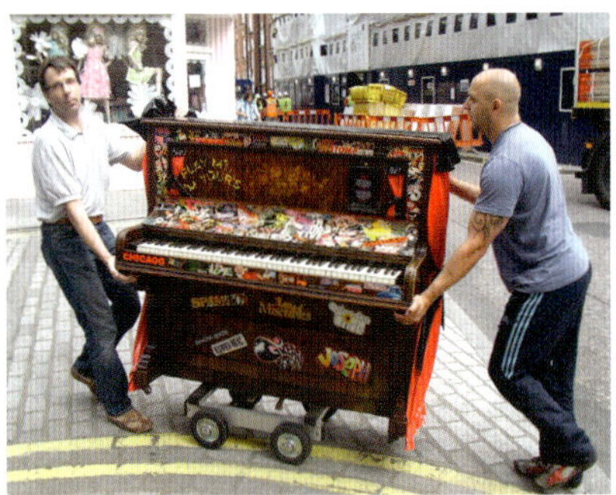

LJ: 'Living in São Paulo, Wesley (right, seated) worked full time, yet still couldn't afford a place to live. Sleeping in the park each night, he taught local children how to play the piano which we'd installed there. Each evening he did a tour of four of the pianos to make sure they were covered for the night.'

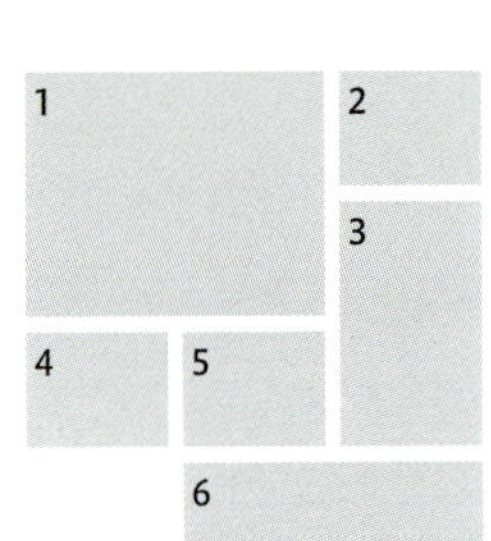

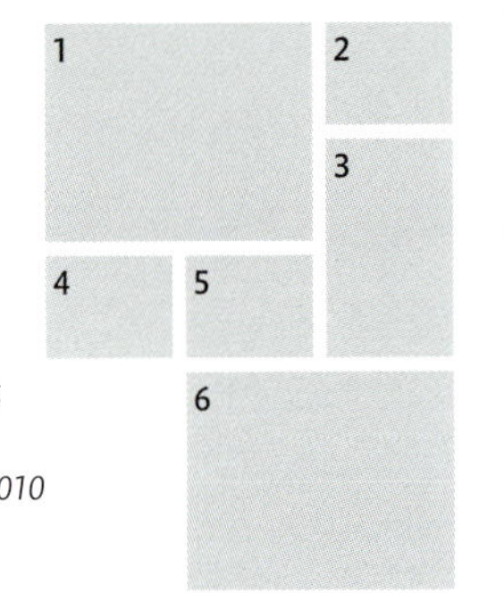

1. *São Paulo, 2008*
2. *Hong Kong, 2015*
3. *Sydney, 2009*
4. *Pécs, Hungary, 2010*
5. *London, 2009*
6. *São Paulo, 2008*

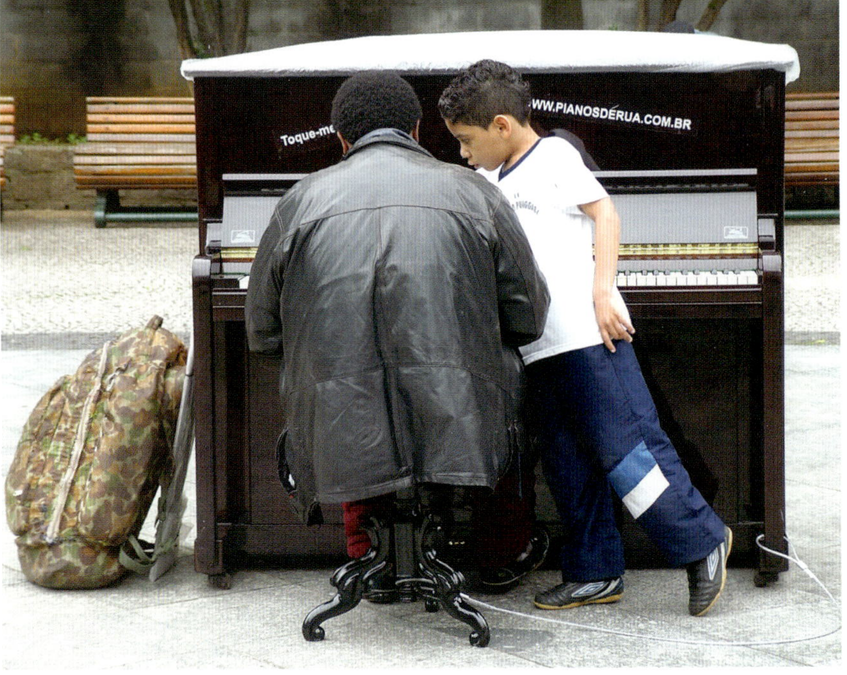

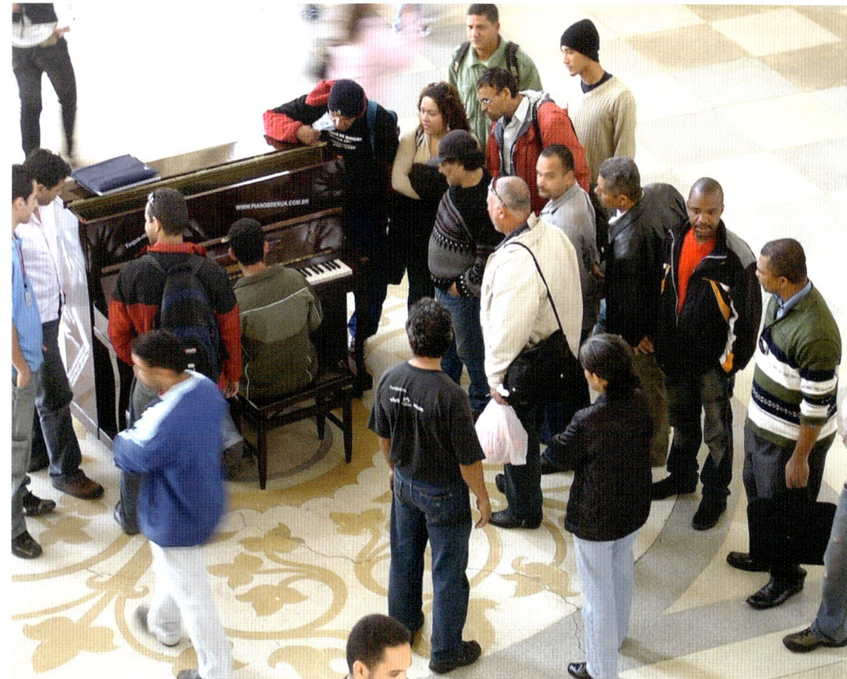

LJ: 'In a train station in São Paulo (right), I came across a girl sitting at a piano with her mother in tears. It turned out the mother had worked as a cleaner for four years so her daughter could have piano lessons on the other side of town. As they couldn't afford their own piano, this was the first time the mother had ever heard her daughter play!'

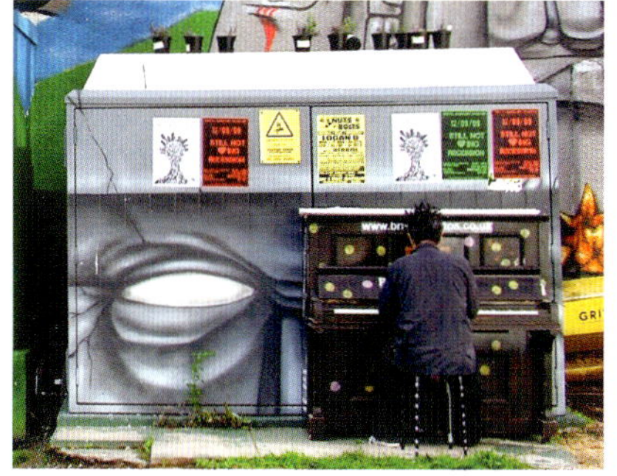

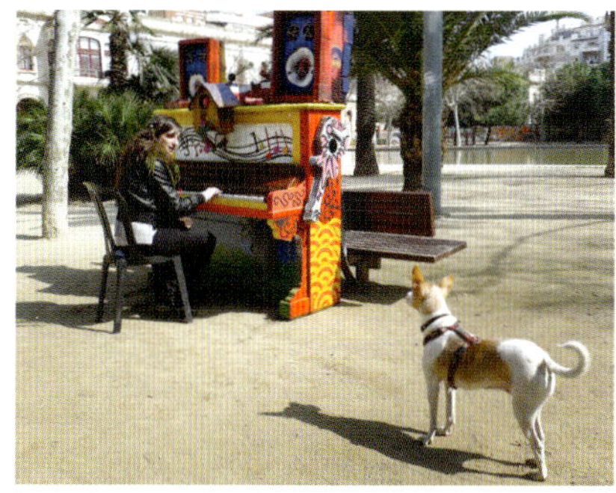

'*Play Me, I'm Yours* created a beautiful and worthy moment for our city, by bringing the street pianos to our city's parks and public spaces. It's things like this that make me extra proud to be a New Yorker, and the endless possibilities represented in these streets.'
Alicia Keys

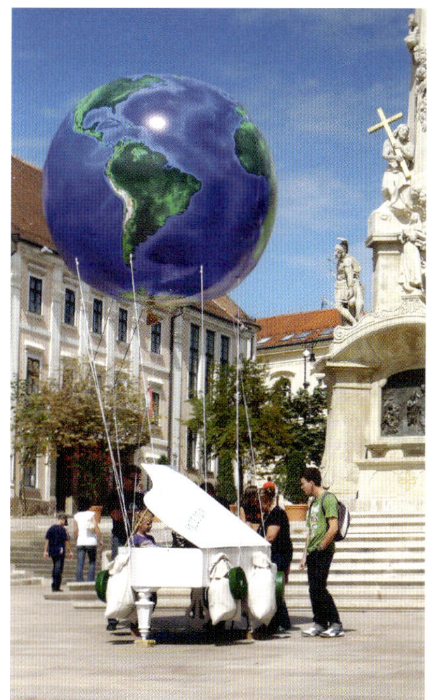

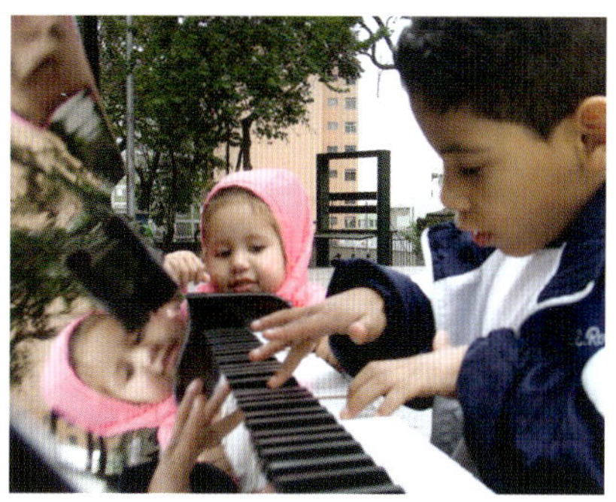

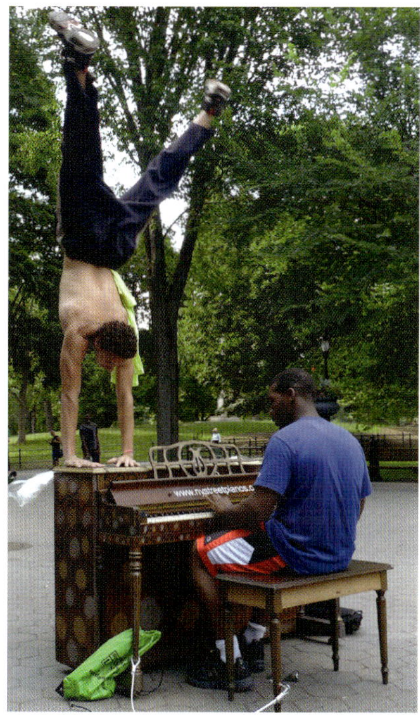

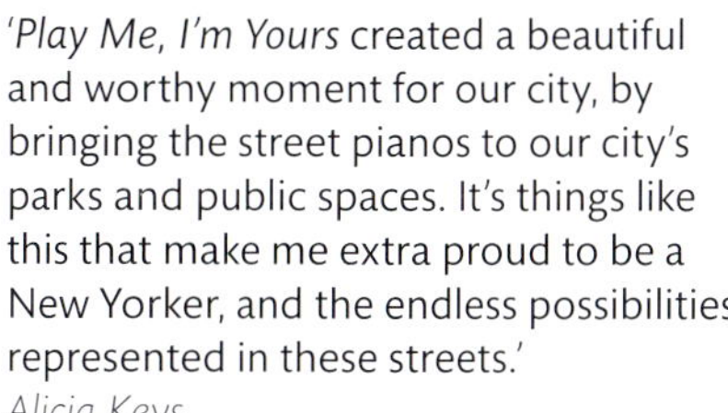

1. *Bristol, 2009*
2. *São Paulo, 2008*
3. *Barcelona, 2010*
4. *Pécs, Hungary, 2010*
5. *São Paulo, 2008*
6. *New York, 2010*
7. *New York, 2010*

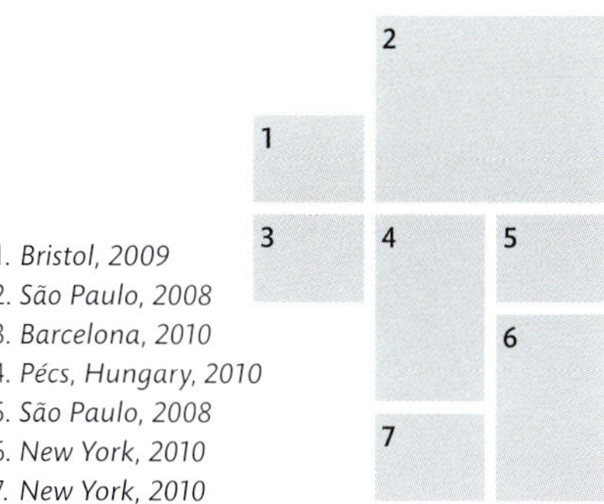

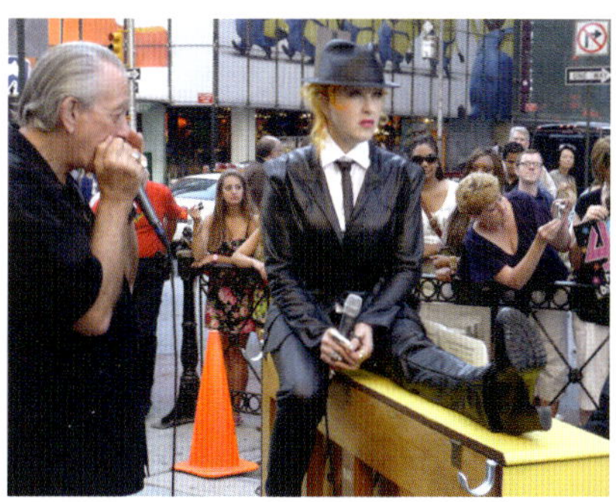

Park and Slide

2014

Enabling the public to navigate the streets of their own city in a new way, *Park and Slide* was a simple architectural intervention and a playful response to the urban landscape.

For one day only, a giant 300-feet waterslide was installed on Park Street, a busy central street in Bristol. Ninety-six thousand people signed up for the chance to get a 'ticket to slide', with just 360 tickets randomly allocated to the lucky participants. Security counted 65,000 people coming to watch, with 60 journalists turning up to cover the event, which led to over 500 news stories worldwide.

Like many of Luke's projects, the installation requires public participation to be activated. The person on the slide becomes the performer, while spectators either side watch on. Cowbells were attached down the length of the fence for spectators to ring as the participants shot down the slide. The end result is a set of collective memories, stories and documentation for people to pass on to others.

Following the event, Luke created an 80-page DIY manual, enabling cities and towns across the world to create their own urban waterslides. Delivering their own slide in Derry-Londonderry, Cancer Research UK raised £60,000. In addition, several commercial companies (not affiliated with Luke) were set up in the USA, Australia and Europe selling urban waterslide experiences.

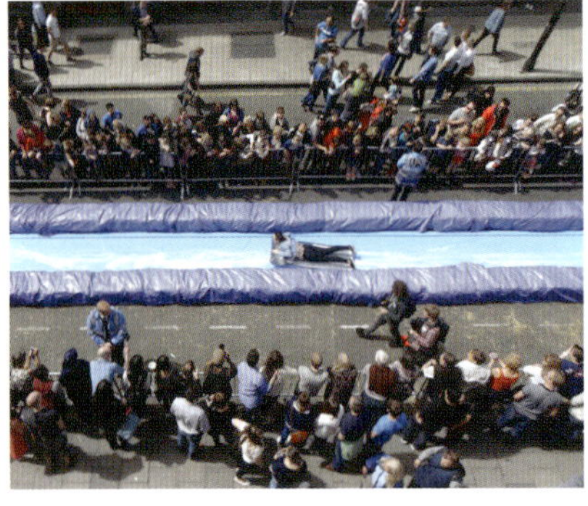

LJ: *The idea for* Park and Slide *came about as I had an office on Park Street and during a heatwave I thought it would be nice to commute home at the end of the day by sliding down the street on a giant waterslide. A massive urban slide transforms the street and asks people to take a fresh look at the potential of their city and the possibilities for transformation. Imagine if there were permanent slides across towns and cities?*

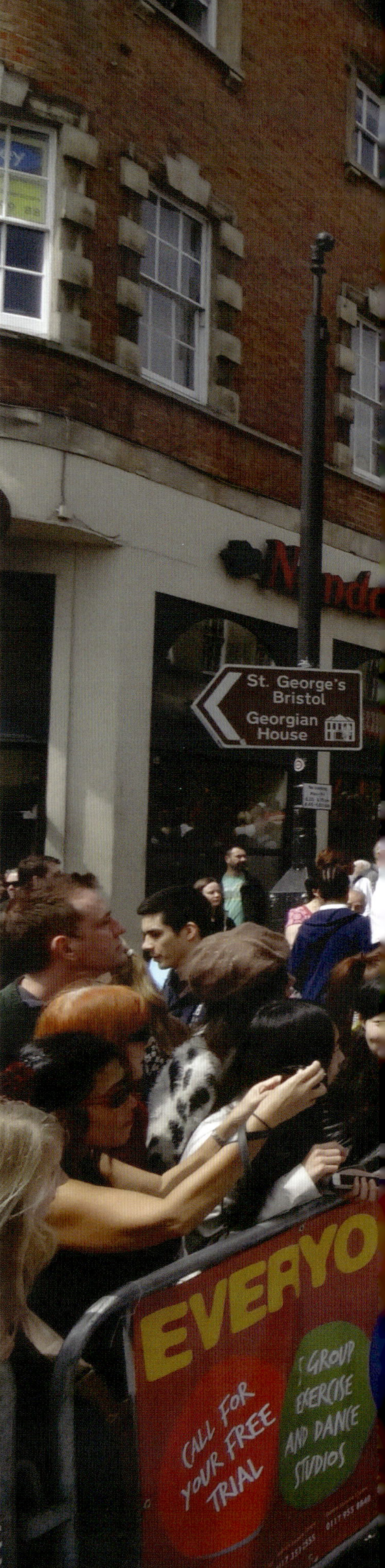

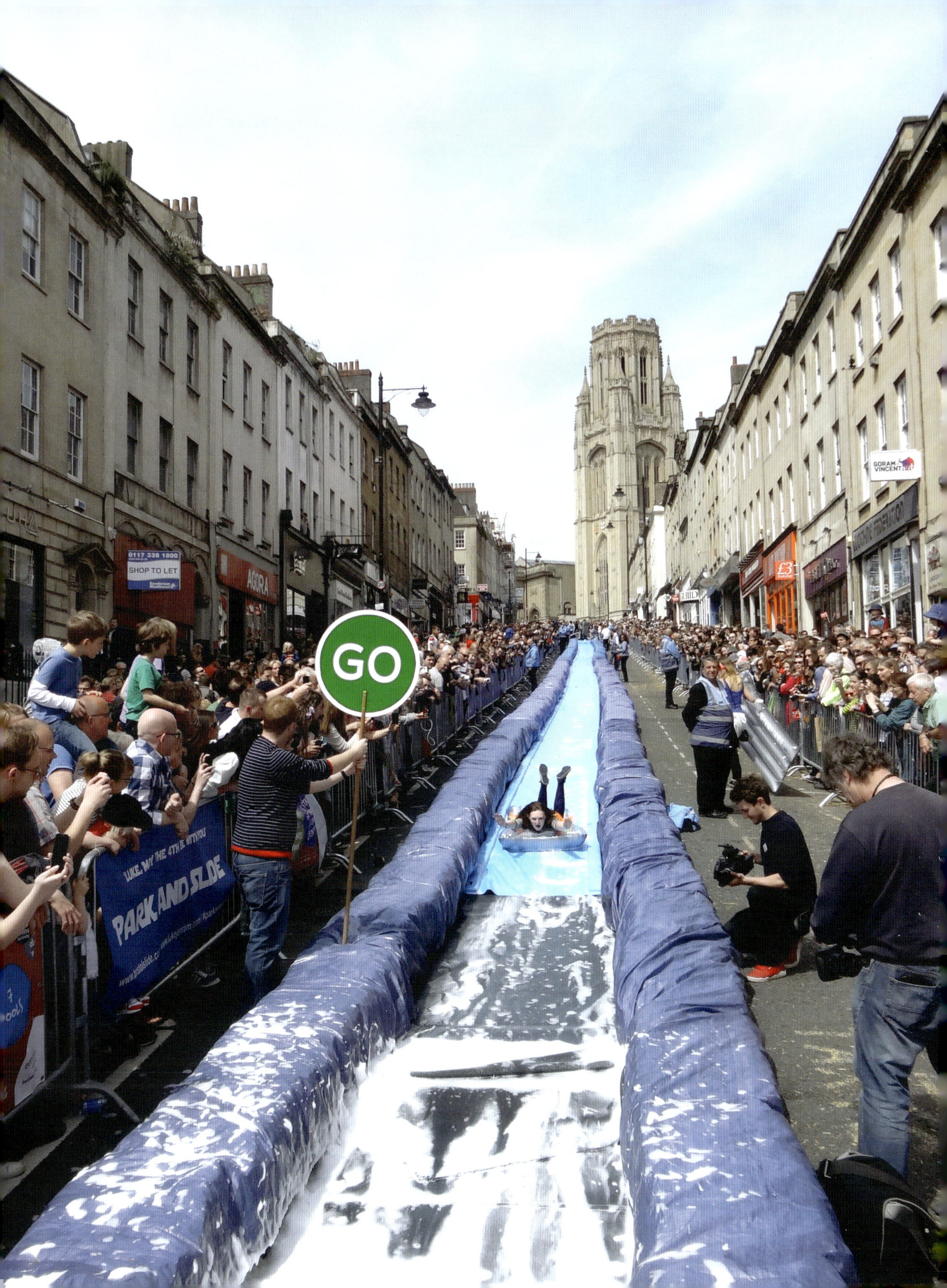

GO
0117 338 1800
SHOP TO LET
AGORA
£3
GORAM VINCENT
LUKE, WAY THE 4TH BE WITH YOU
PARK AND SLIDE

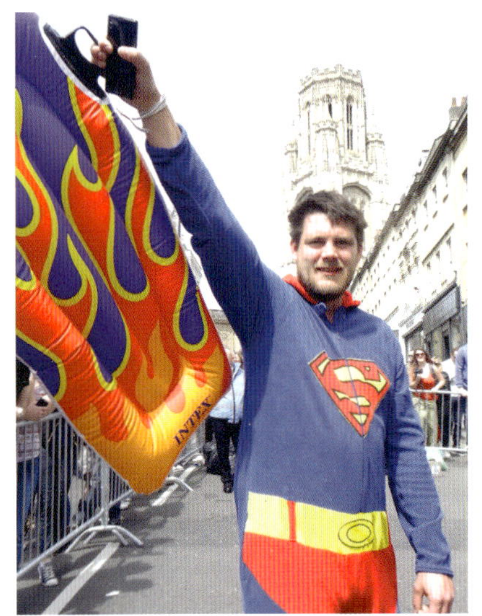
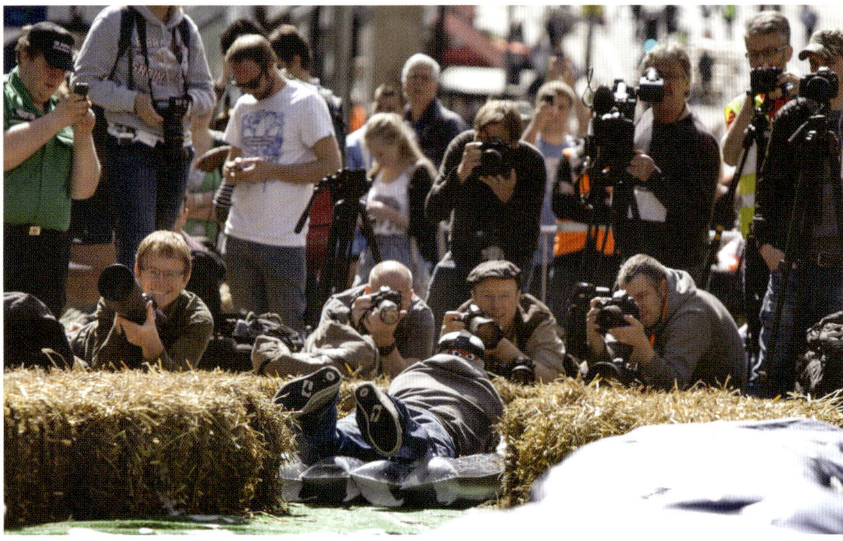
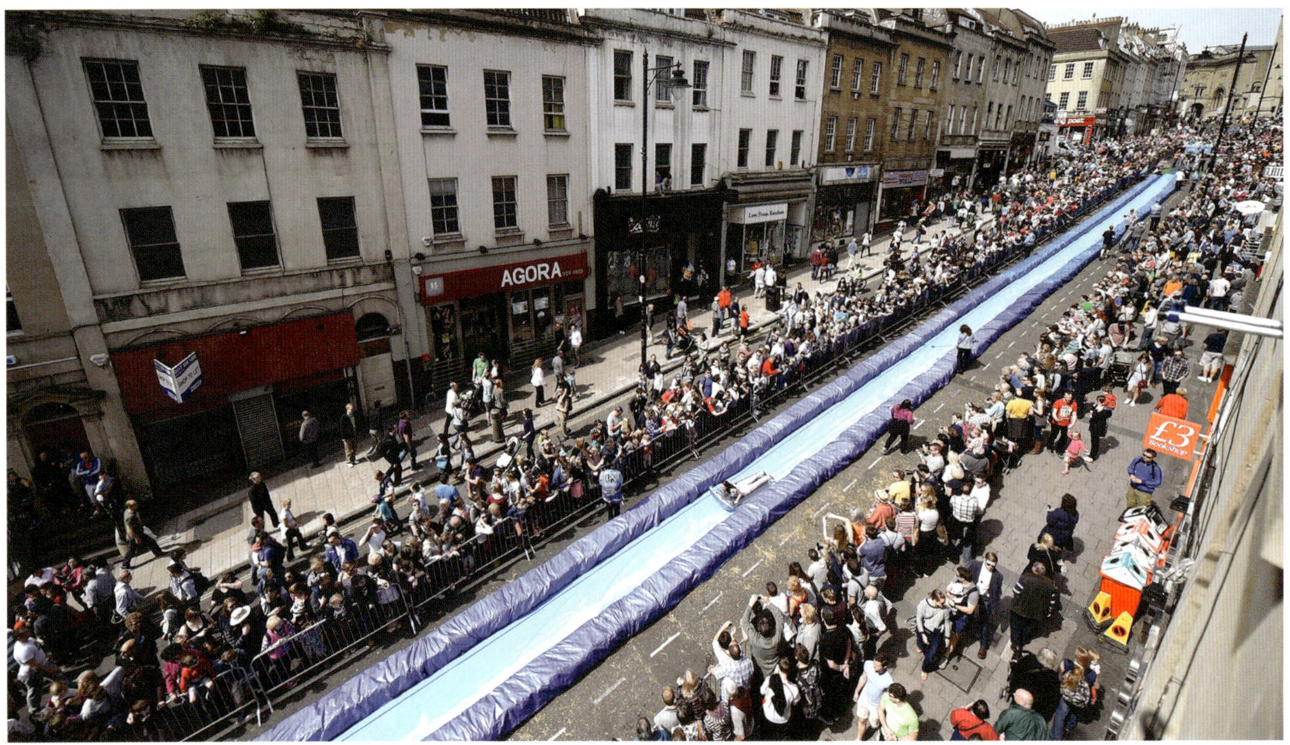

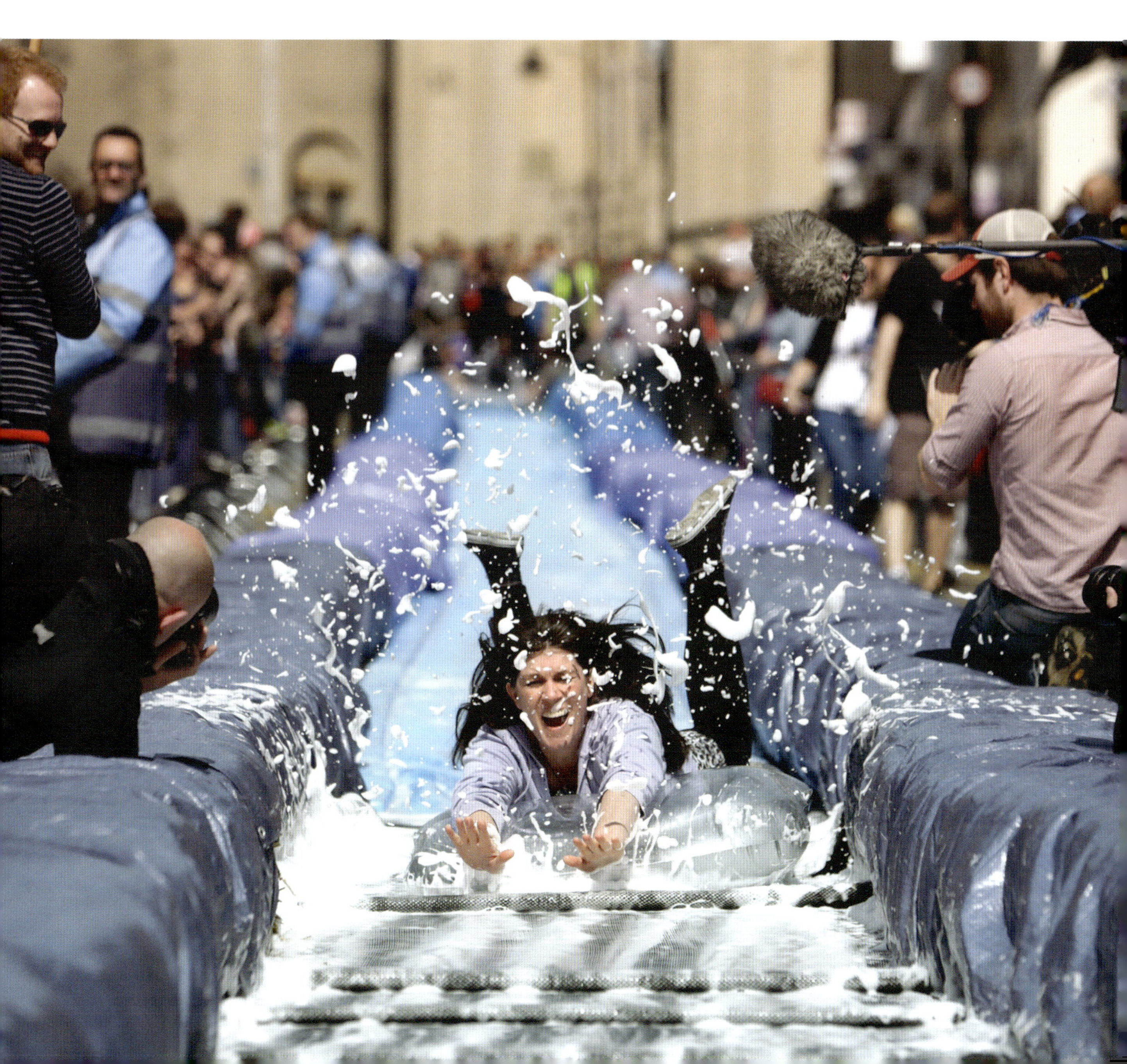

Lullaby
2013–2015

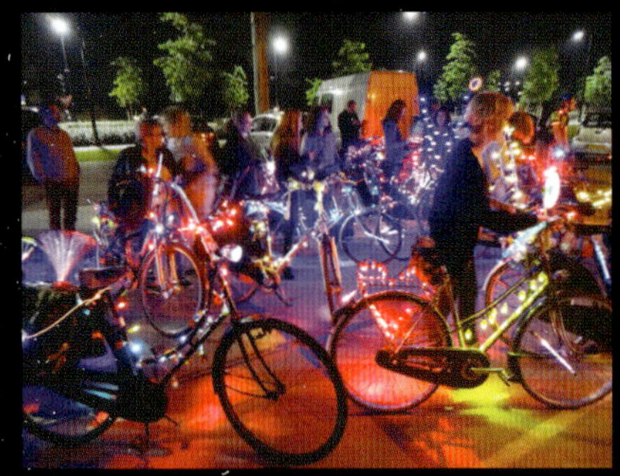

Tilburg, Netherlands, 2014

LJ: *The vision for* Lullaby *came from an early childhood memory, when each Christmas the local bus company would decorate a double-decker bus with lights then drive around villages, playing distorted carol music through tannoy speakers. Seen at night, from the other side of the valley, it was like aliens were landing.*

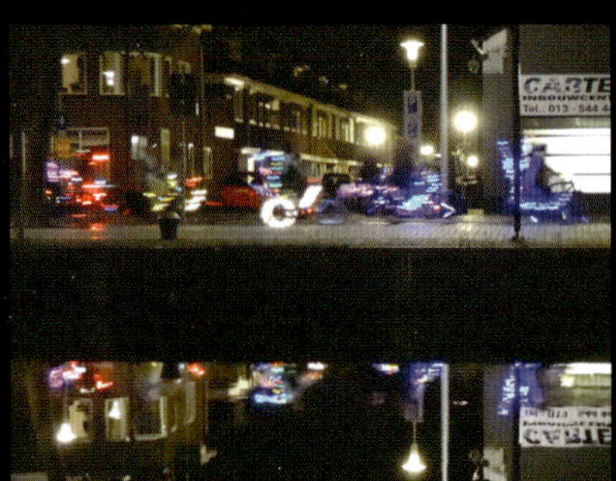

Tilburg, Netherlands, 2014

Lullaby is the first artwork Luke has made specifically for families with young children. As a parent, he is particularly aware that a child's bedtime is a very special and fragile time of day. At dusk, when the suburbs are quiet and empty, serene music can be heard drifting down the street and a shoal of twinkling lights is seen in the distance. Only as they pass their homes do people realise that the music is coming from speakers attached to dozens of LED lit, decorated bikes. *Lullaby* is a gift to a city, a surround-sound illuminated artwork, created by its own citizens and delivered to people's doors. In Derry-Londonderry residents from both sides of the political divide delivered a *Lullaby* to those in the opposite community.

Lullaby stems from Luke's past research into sleep and his other sleep-based projects *Sky Orchestra* and *Dream Director*. As with other artworks such as *Play Me, I'm Yours* and *Park and Slide*, the project requires the active participation of people to be complete.

Originally commissioned by Sustrans, *Lullaby* performances have taken place in Bristol and Portland; Tilburg; Derry-Londonderry and Perth, Australia. The musical score for *Lullaby* was composed by Bristol-based musician Andy Taylor.

▶ *Derry-Londonderry, 2015*

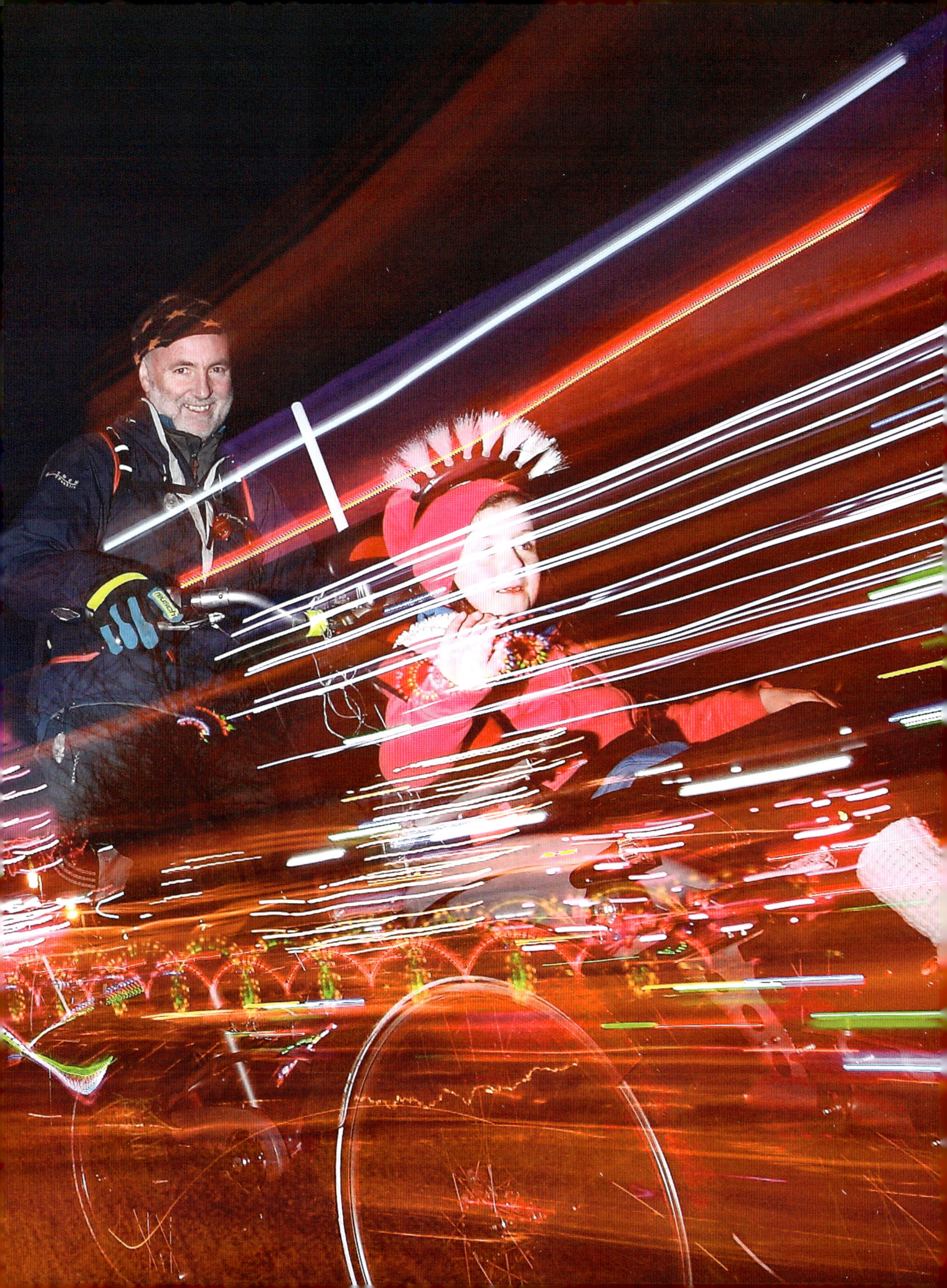

Withdrawn

2015

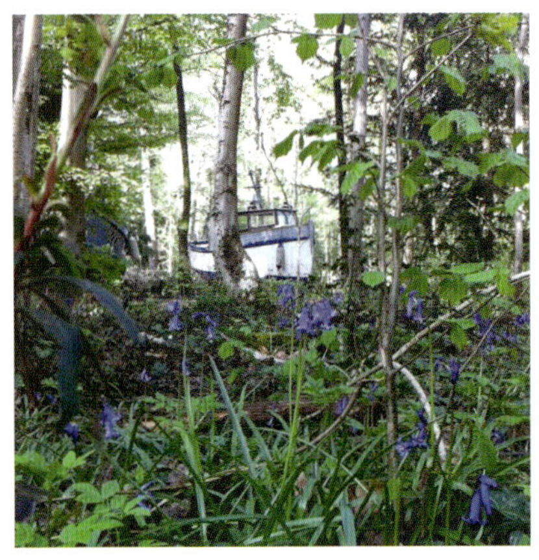

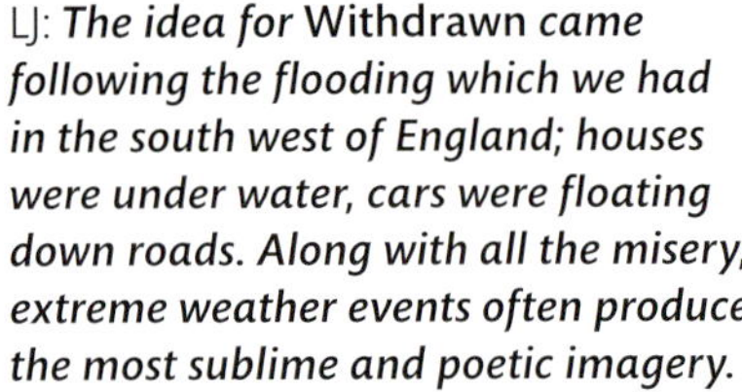

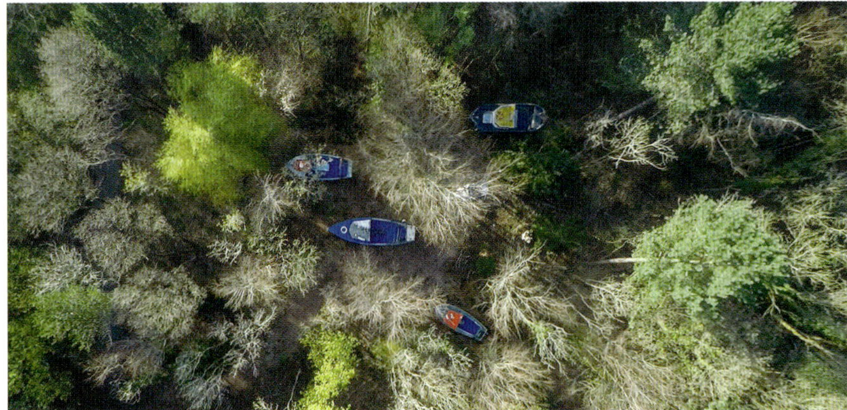

LJ: *The idea for* Withdrawn *came following the flooding which we had in the south west of England; houses were under water, cars were floating down roads. Along with all the misery, extreme weather events often produce the most sublime and poetic imagery.*

Located in the depths of Leigh Woods in Bristol, *Withdrawn* was an installation of abandoned fishing boats, all pointing the same way as if turned by the tide or moving together. The flotilla was an unexpected encounter for visitors to the woodland, with the wind in the trees reminiscent of the sound of waves. As well as providing a surreal and memorable experience, the artwork also raised issues around climate change, extreme weather, falling fish stocks, and our impact on the marine environment. The boats were used as a venue for a programme of special events including marine and environmental discussions, sound installations, theatrical perform-ances, and interactive workshops, staged both during daytime and at night.

At the end of the project all of the boats were given away and repurposed. One boat was given to a man who planned to turn it into a pirate ship for a play park in the village of Norwood Green. He only told the local council about his intentions when the boat turned up. The council committee decided not to accept the boat, that is until the entire village arrived, all dressed as pirates, with banners protesting the decision.

Withdrawn was commissioned by the National Trust's Trust New Art programme and was delivered in partnership with Forestry Commission England's Forest Art Works programme as part of *Bristol 2015*.

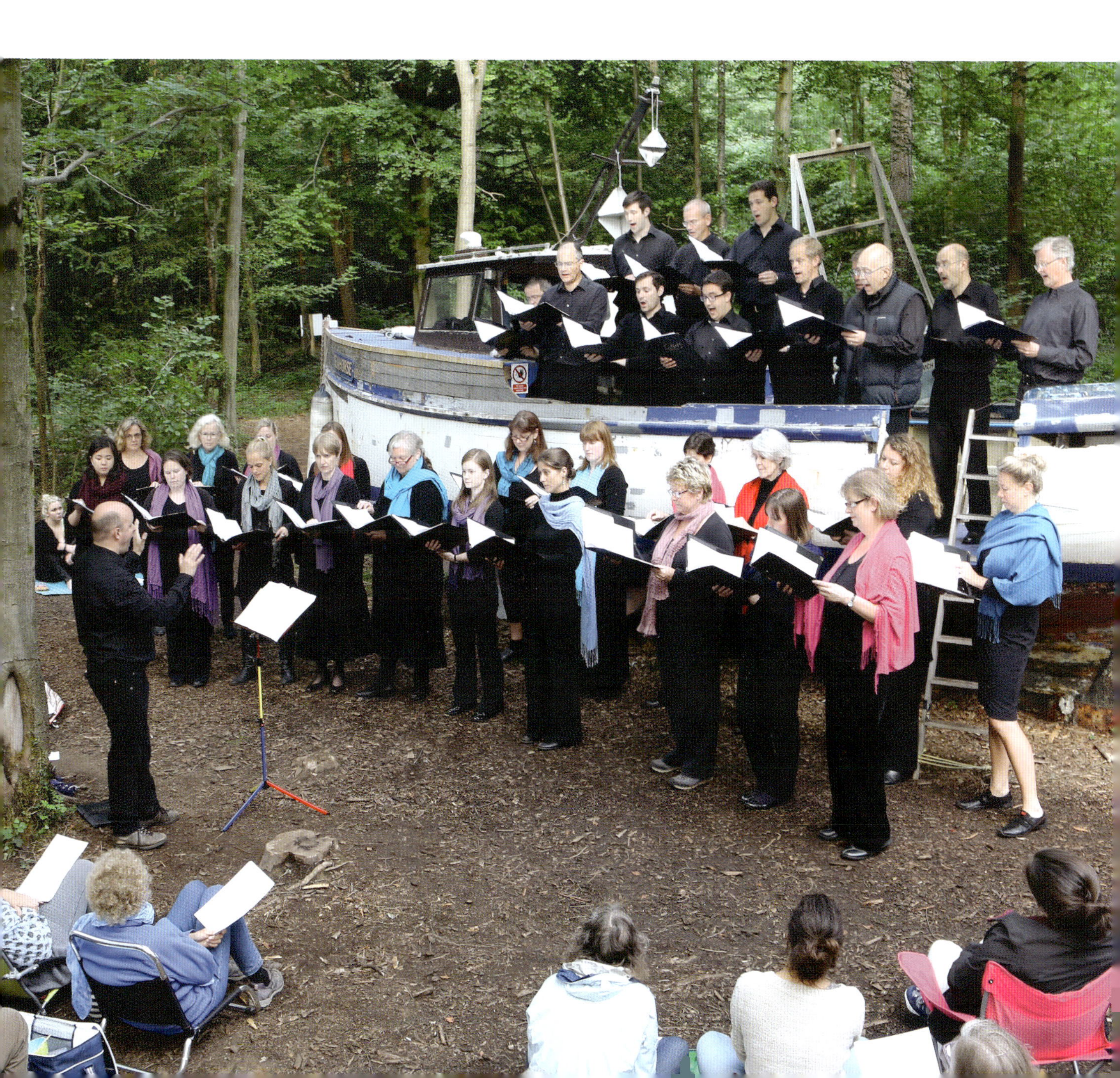

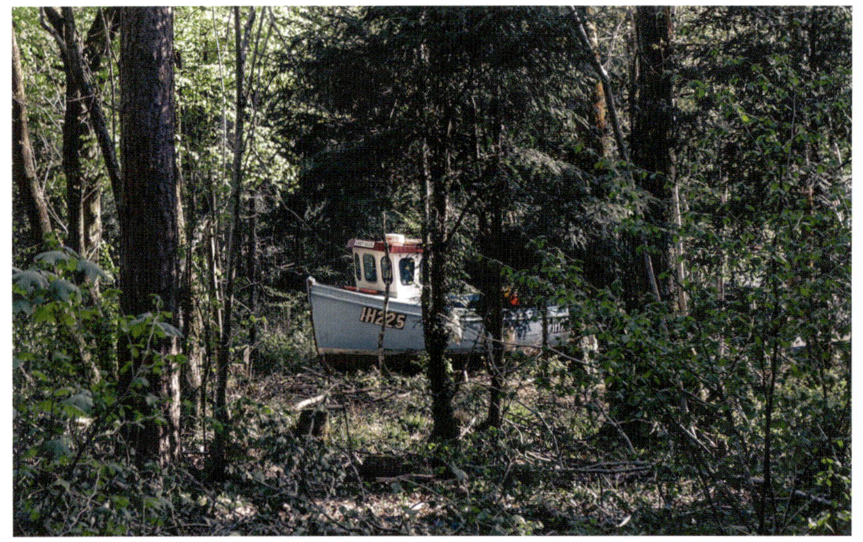

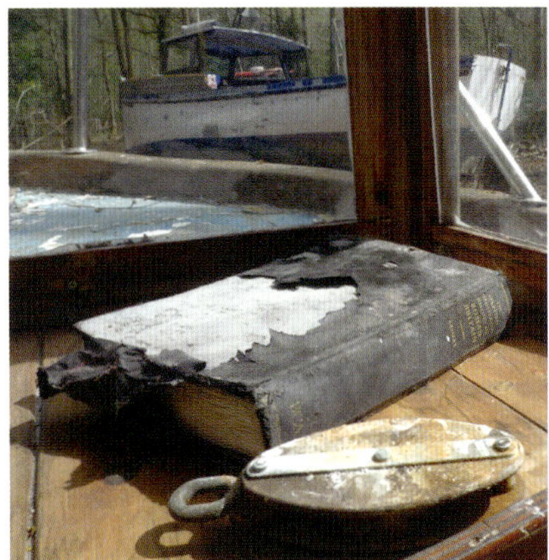

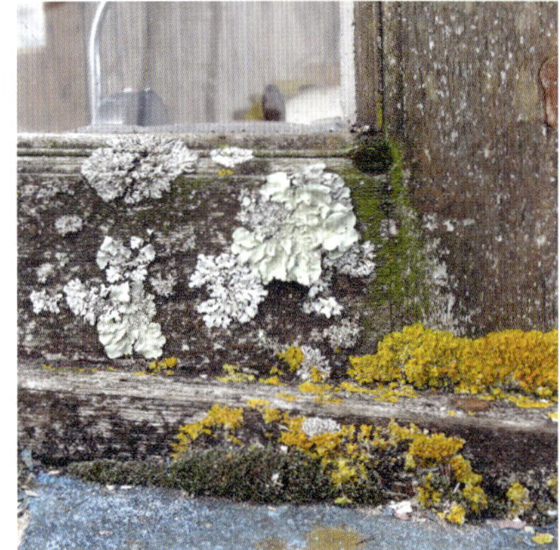

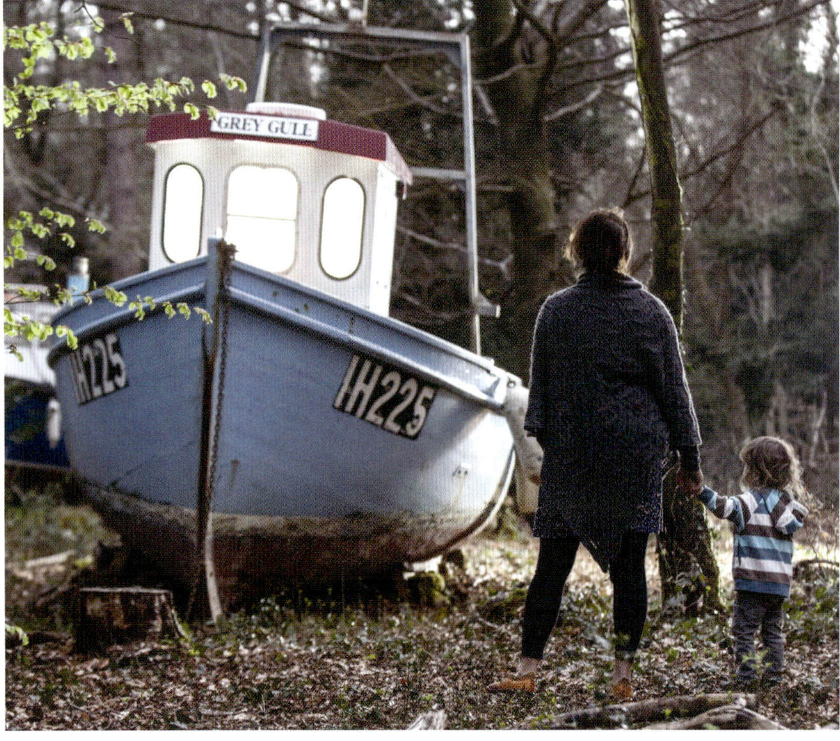

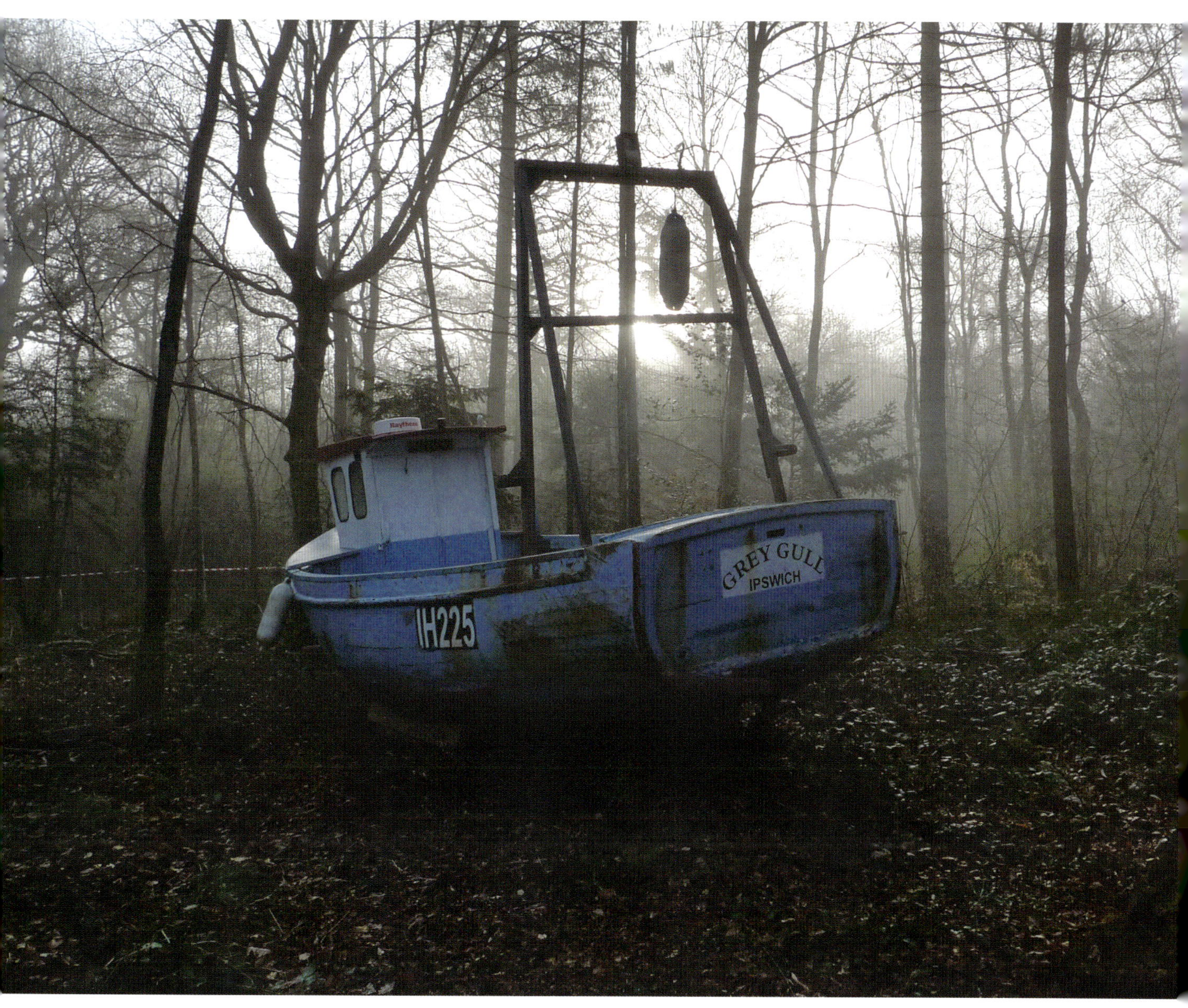
GREY GULL
IPSWICH
IH225
Raytheon

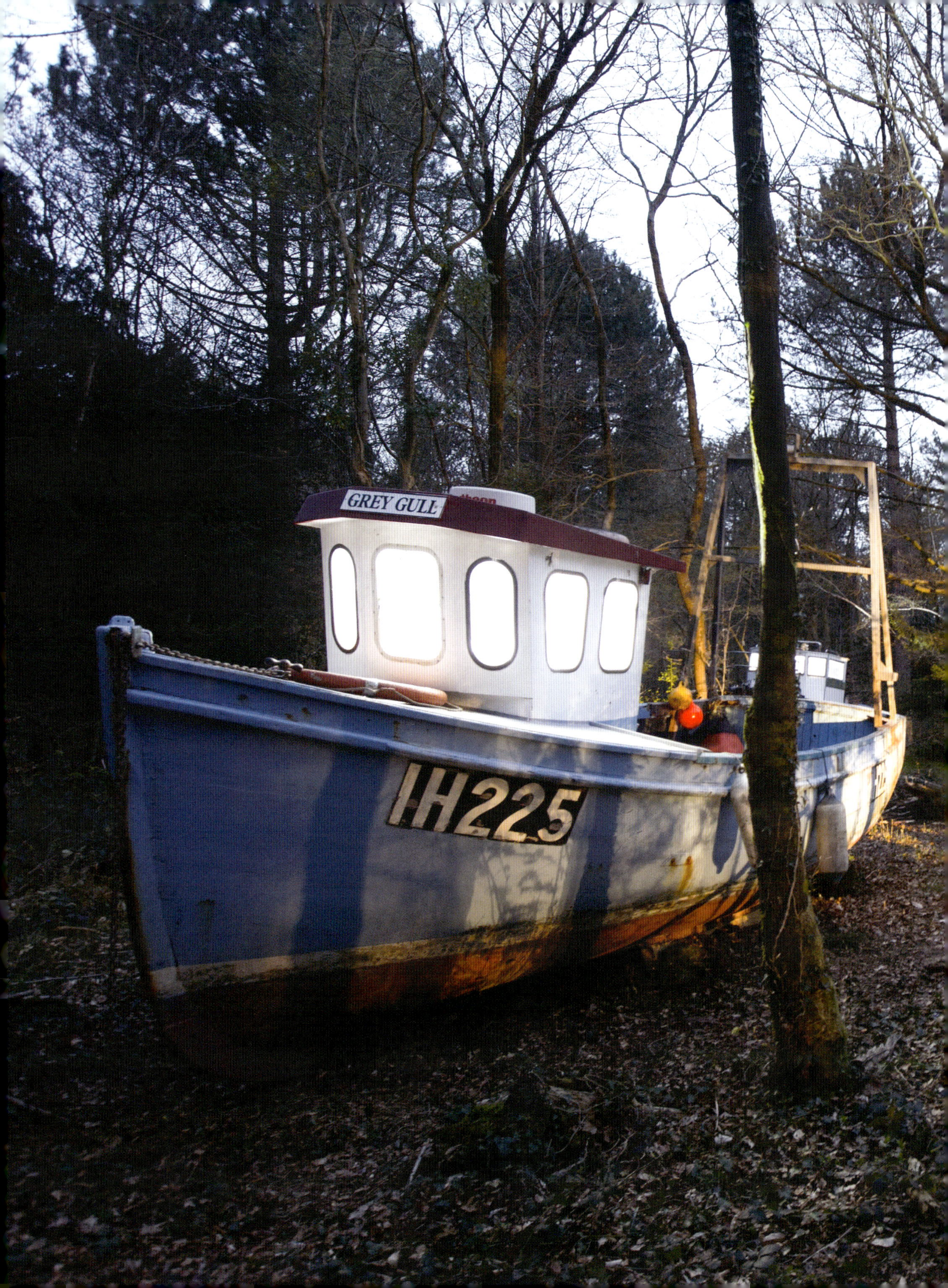

GREY GULL
IH225

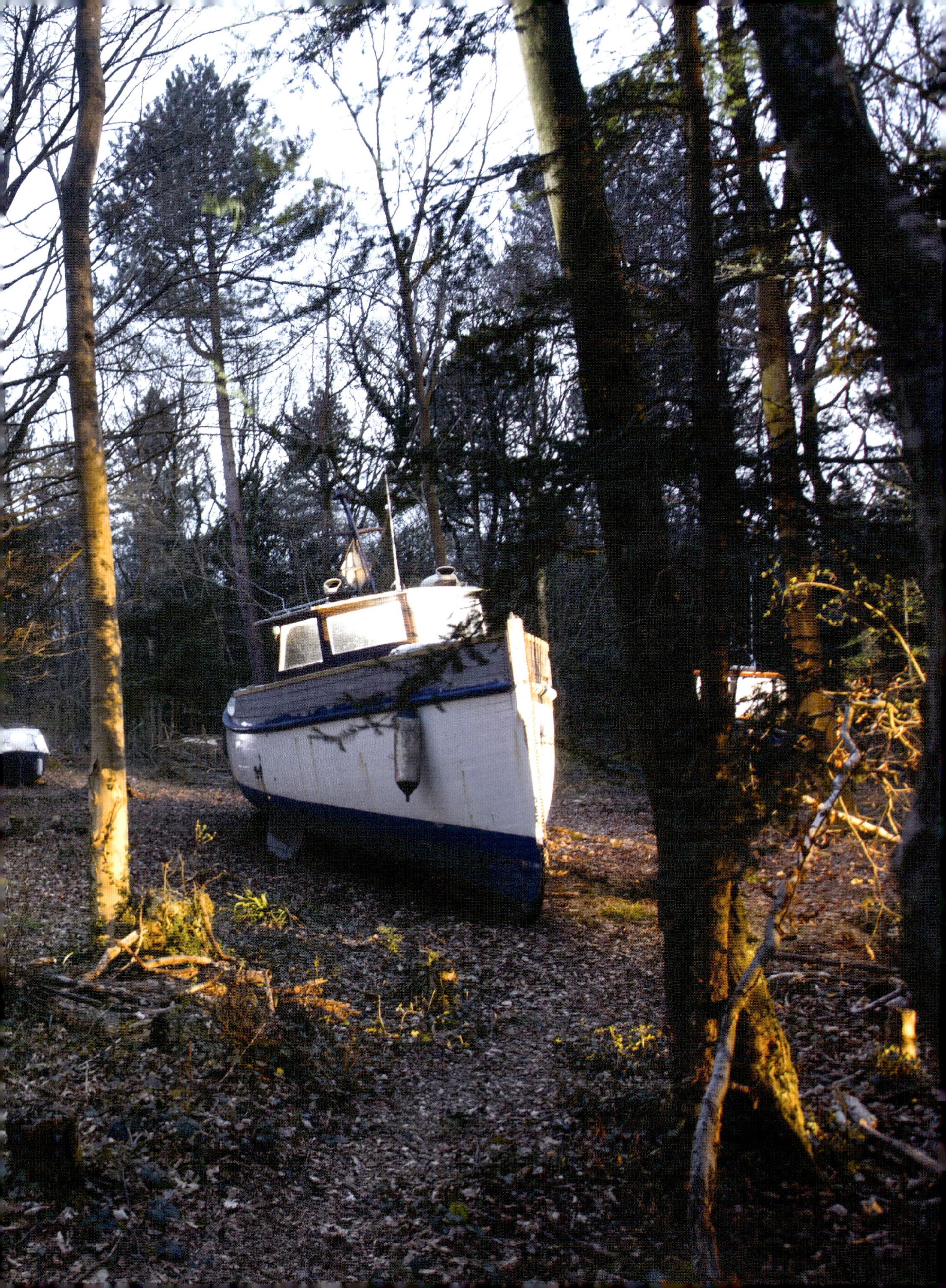

Museum of the Moon

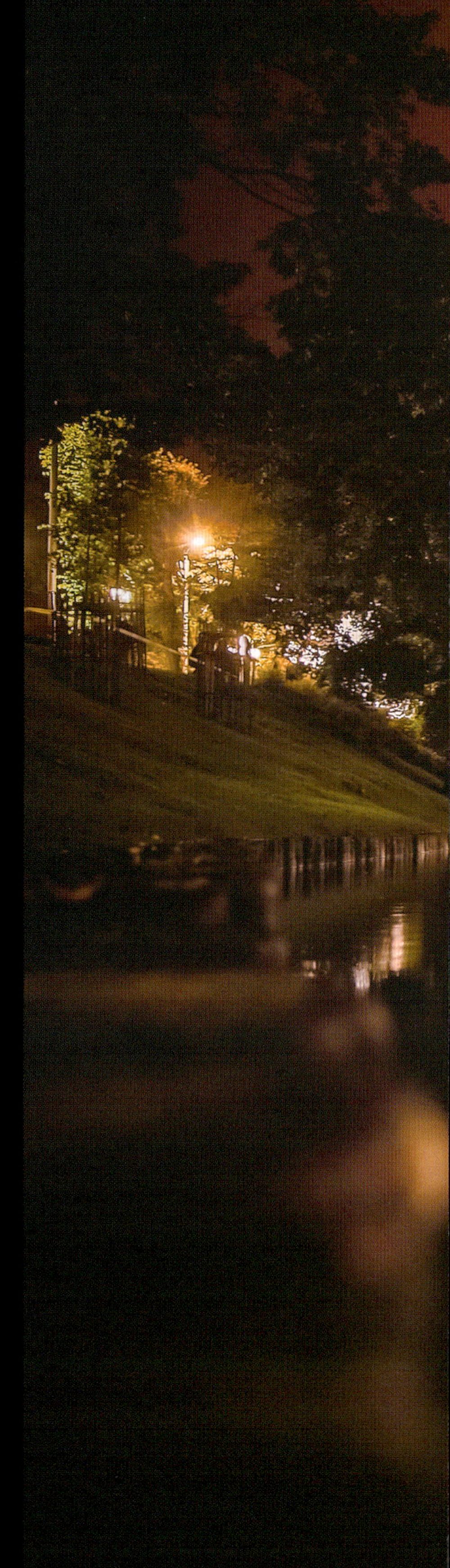

Measuring seven metres in diameter, the Moon features 120dpi detailed NASA imagery of the lunar surface. At an approximate scale of 1:500,000, each centimetre of the internally lit spherical sculpture represents five kilometres of the Moon's surface.

The installation is a fusion of lunar imagery, 'moonlight' and surround-sound composition created by BAFTA and Ivor Novello award-winning composer Dan Jones. Over its lifetime, *Museum of the Moon* will be presented in a number of different ways, both indoors and outdoors, altering the experience and interpretation of the artwork. Each venue that it travels to programmes a bespoke series of lunar-inspired events to take place beneath it. As the Moon travels from place to place it gathers new musical compositions and an ongoing collection of personal responses, stories and mythologies, as well as highlighting the latest moon science.

From the beginning of human history, the Moon has acted as a 'cultural mirror' to our beliefs, understanding and ways of seeing. Over the centuries, it has been interpreted as a god, a planet, and even as a timekeeper and calendar. Different cultures have their own historical, social, scientific and religious relationships to the Moon. *Museum of the Moon* allows us to observe and contemplate these cultural similarities and differences around the world.

Museum of the Moon has been co-commissioned by a number of creative organisations brought together by Luke Jerram and *Norfolk & Norwich Festival*, including *Greenwich+Docklands International Festival*, *Brighton Festival*, Without Walls, *Cork Midsummer Festival*, At-Bristol, *Lakes Alive*, Provinciaal Domein Dommelhof, *Les Tombées de la Nuit*, Rennes, and Kimmel Center for the Performing Arts. Created in partnership with the UK Space Agency, University of Bristol and the Association for Science and Discovery Centres.

LJ: *It's been wonderful to witness people's response to the artwork. Many people spend hours with the Moon exploring its every detail. Visitors even lie down and 'moon-bathe'.*

'When I first came into the room, and saw the Moon, I cried.'
Anna, Bristol

'Did you make the real Moon as well?'
Harry (age 8), Leicester

▶ *White Night, Riga, 2017*

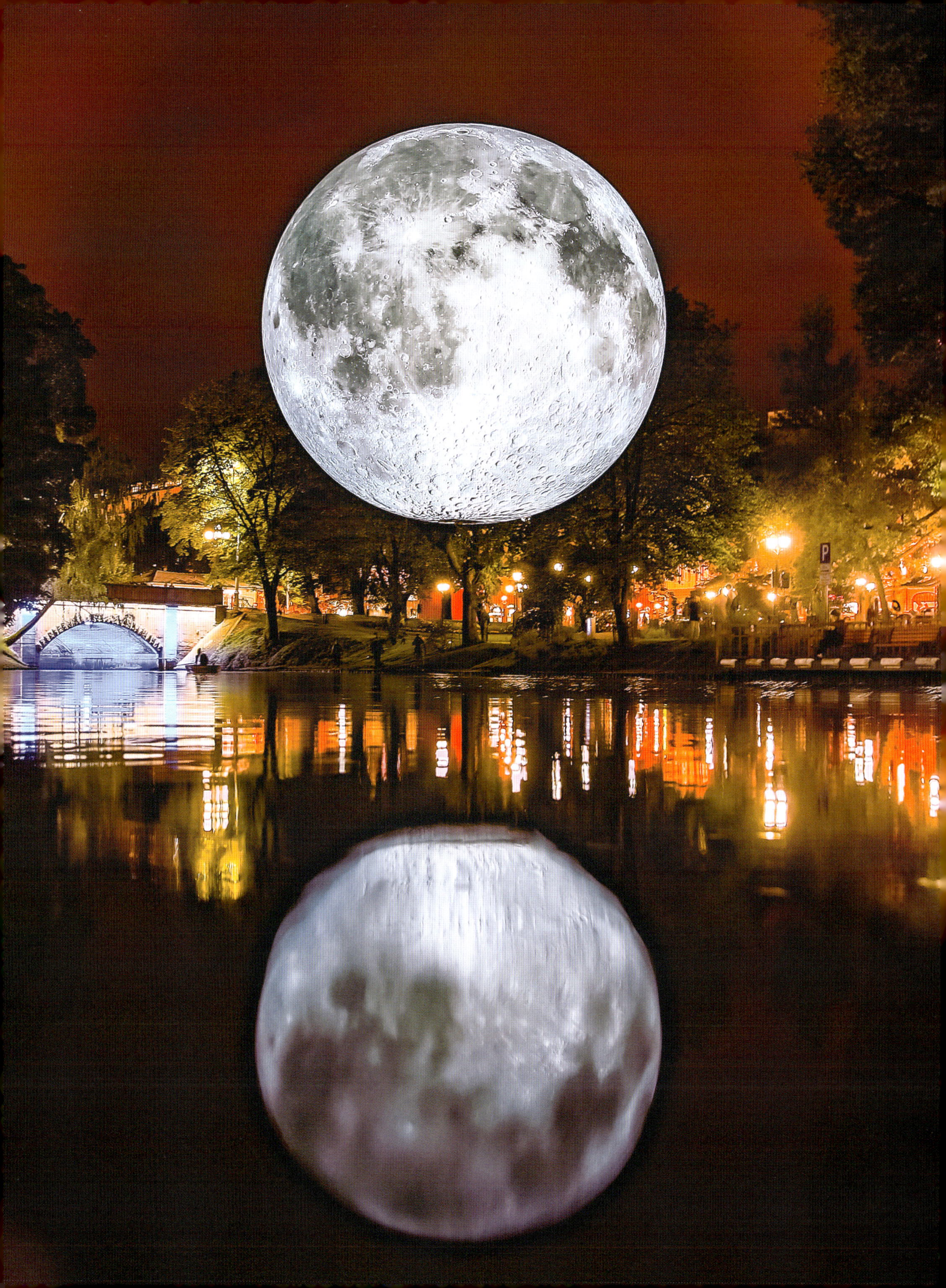

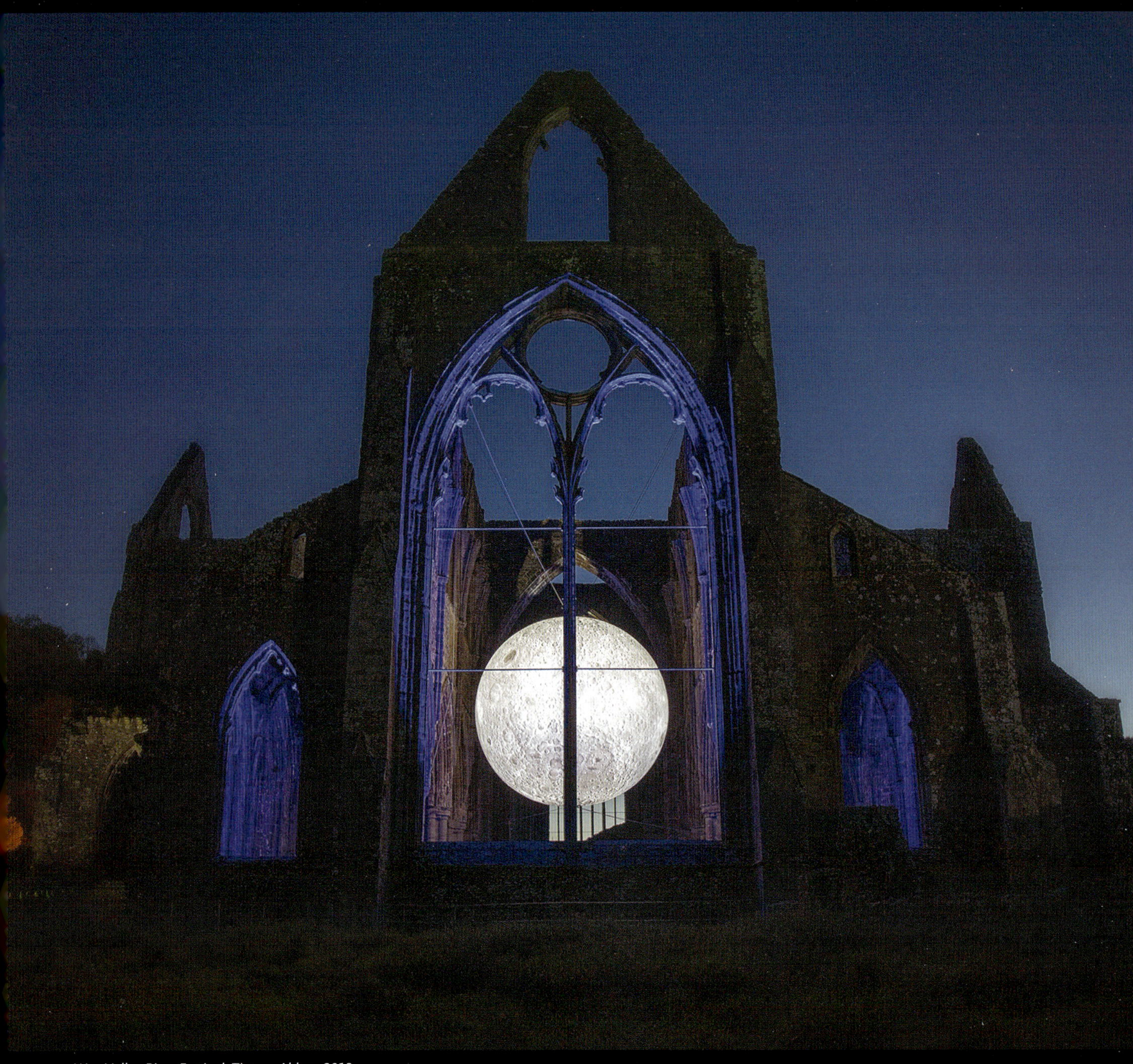

Wye Valley River Festival, Tintern Abbey, 2018

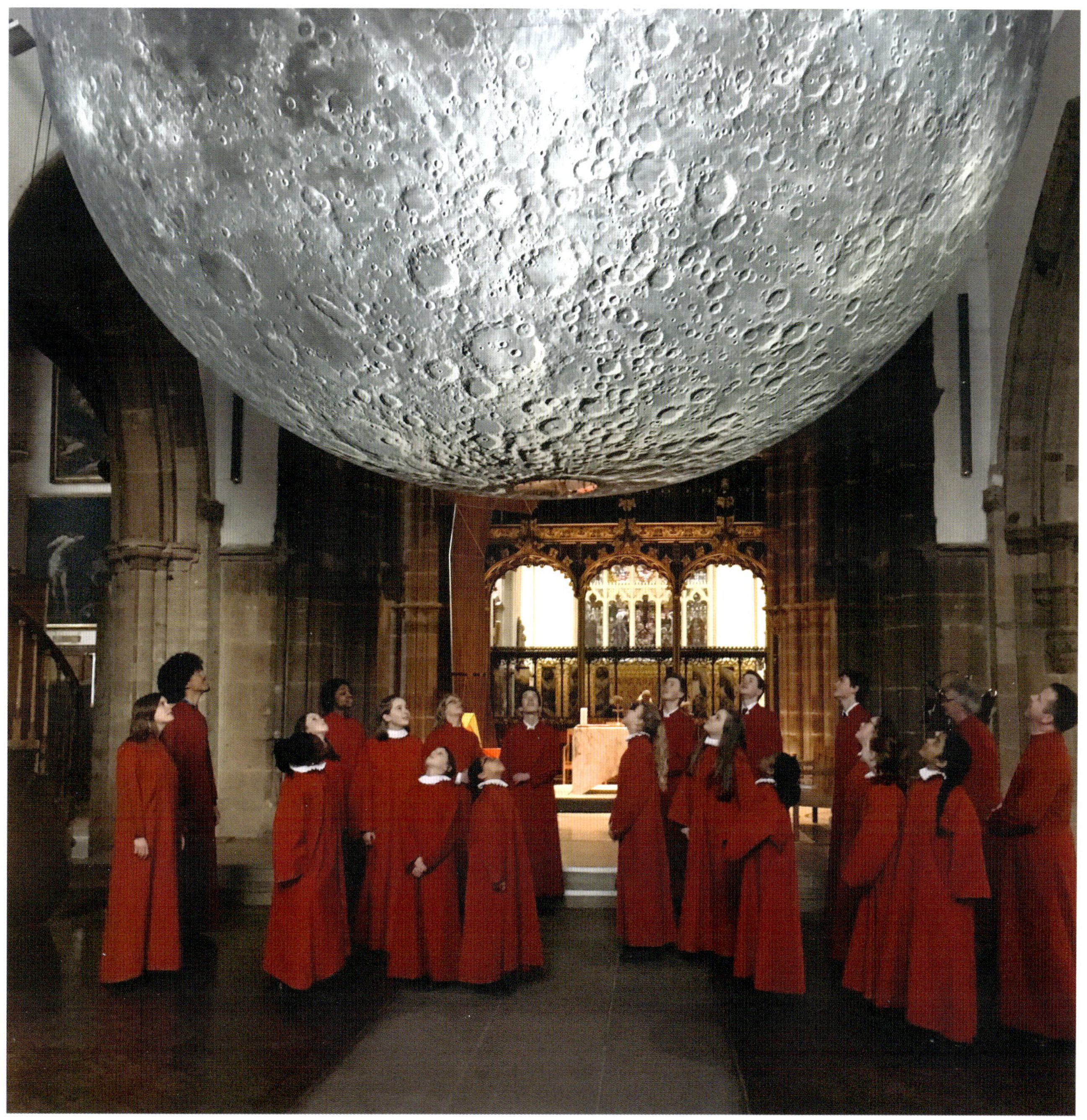

British Science Week, Leicester Cathedral, 2018

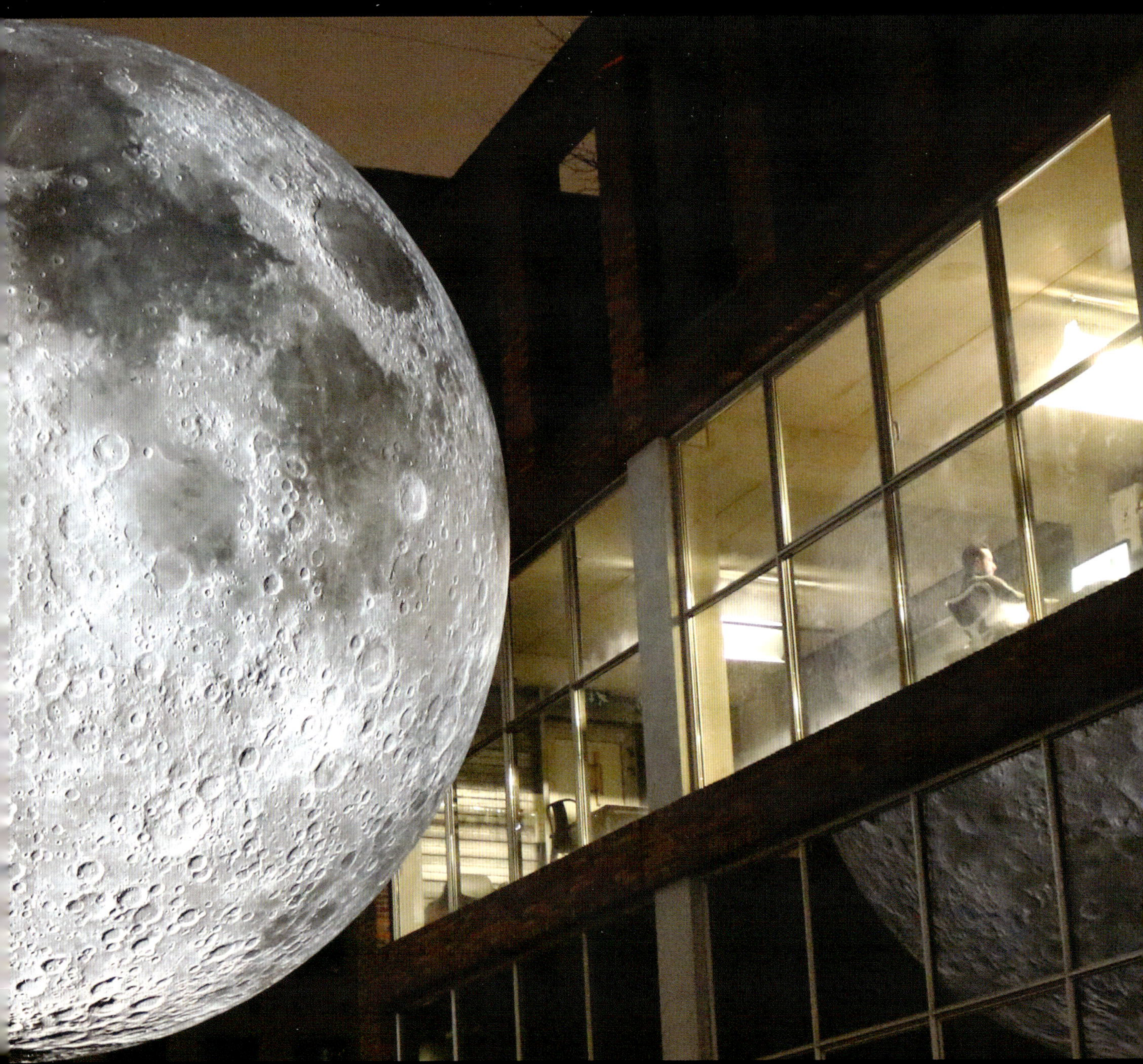

TEC ART, Rotterdam, 2017

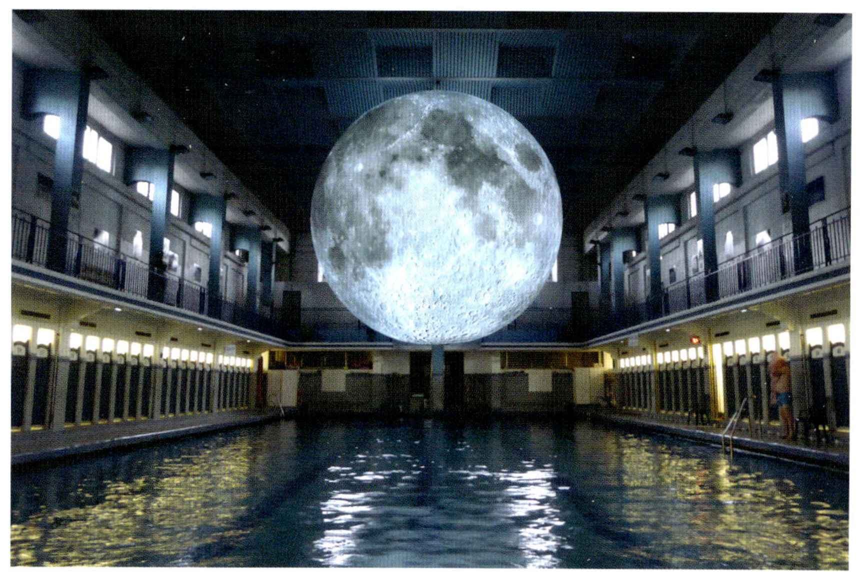

Les Tombées de la Nuit, Rennes, 2017

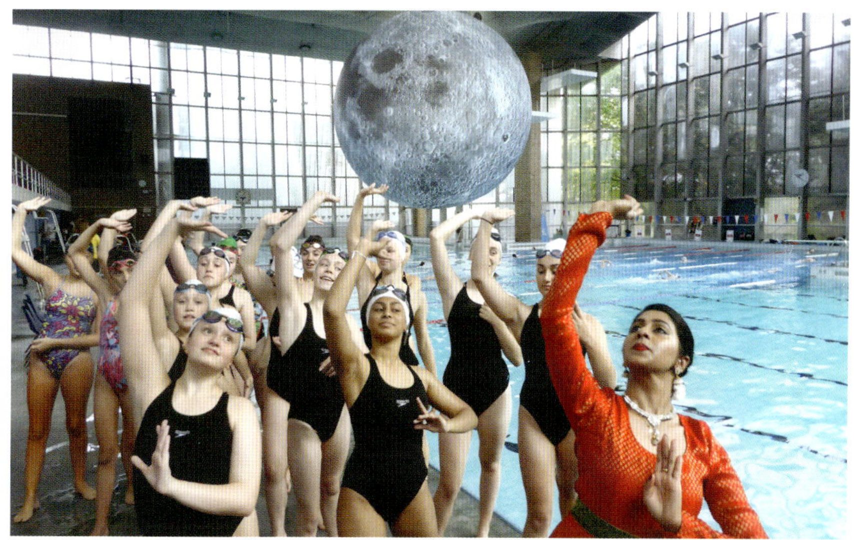

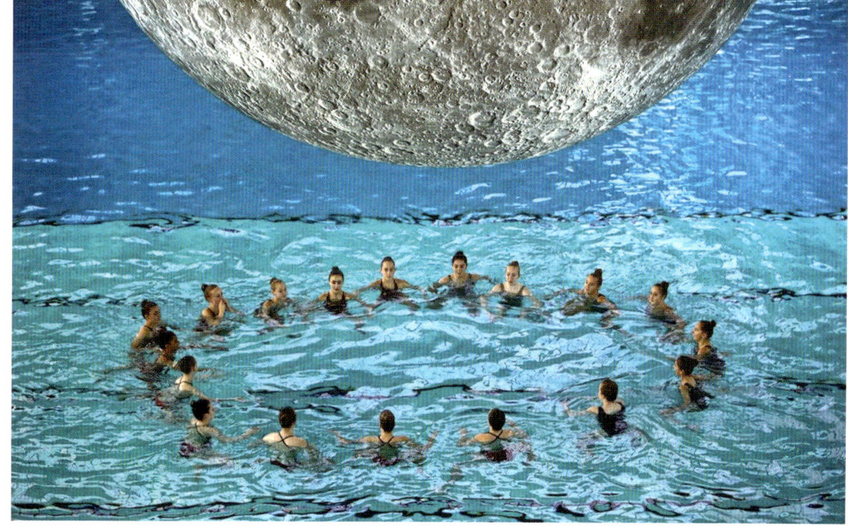

Festival of Imagineers, Coventry, 2017

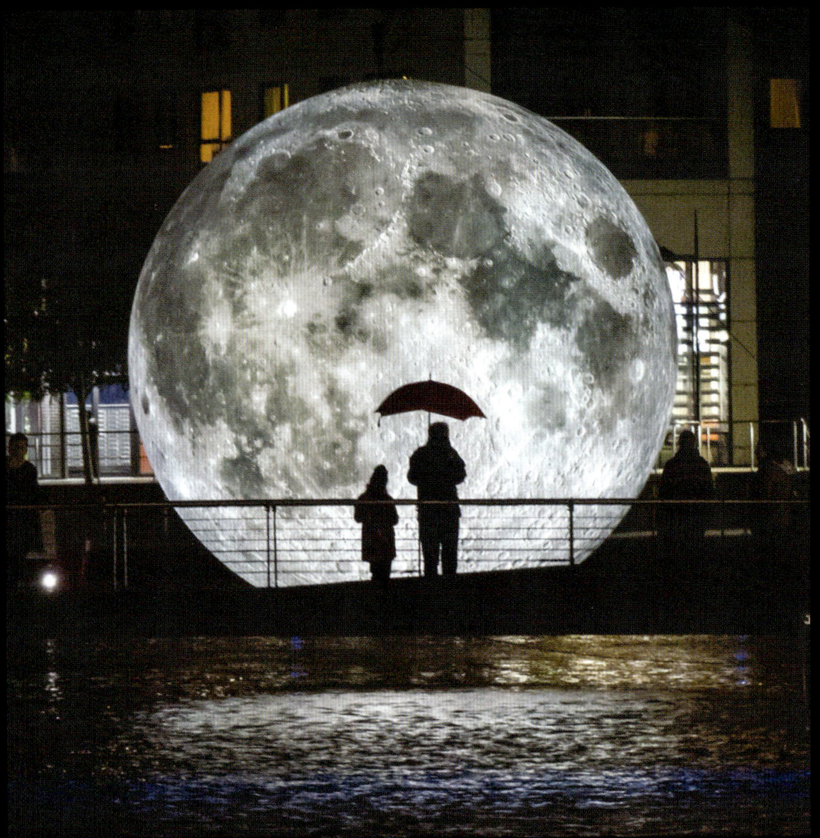
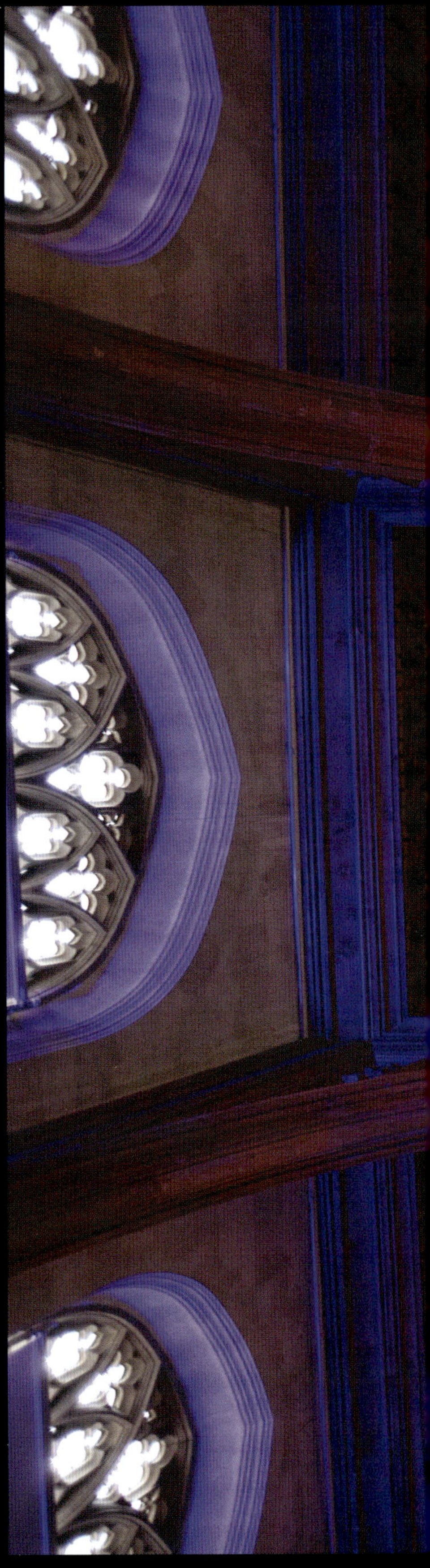

Light Night, Leeds, 2017

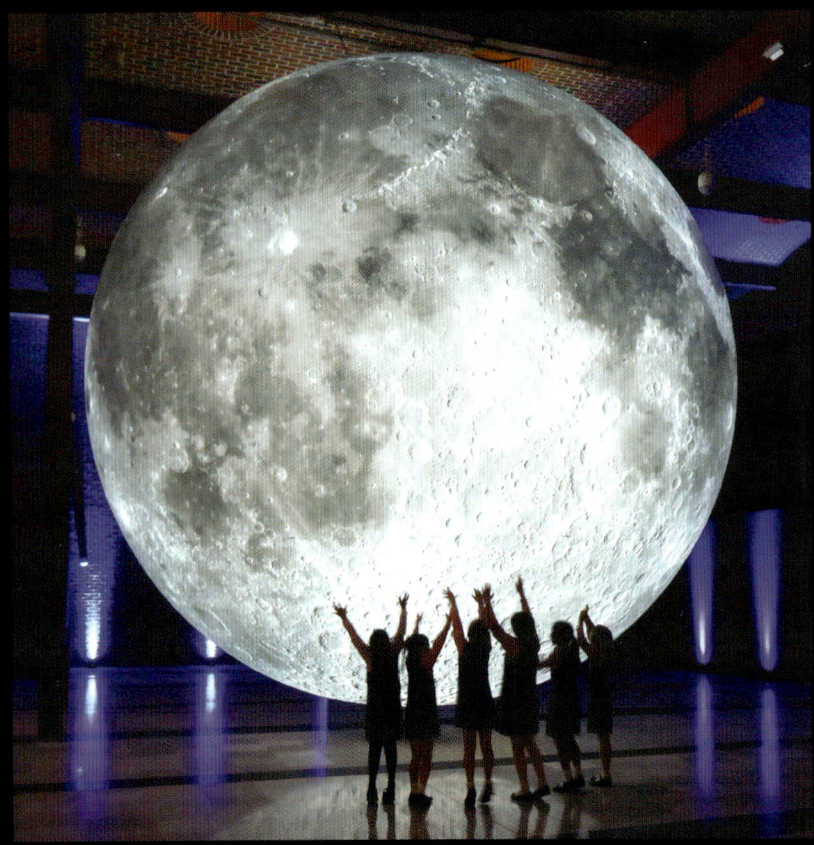

Cork Midsummer Festival, 2017

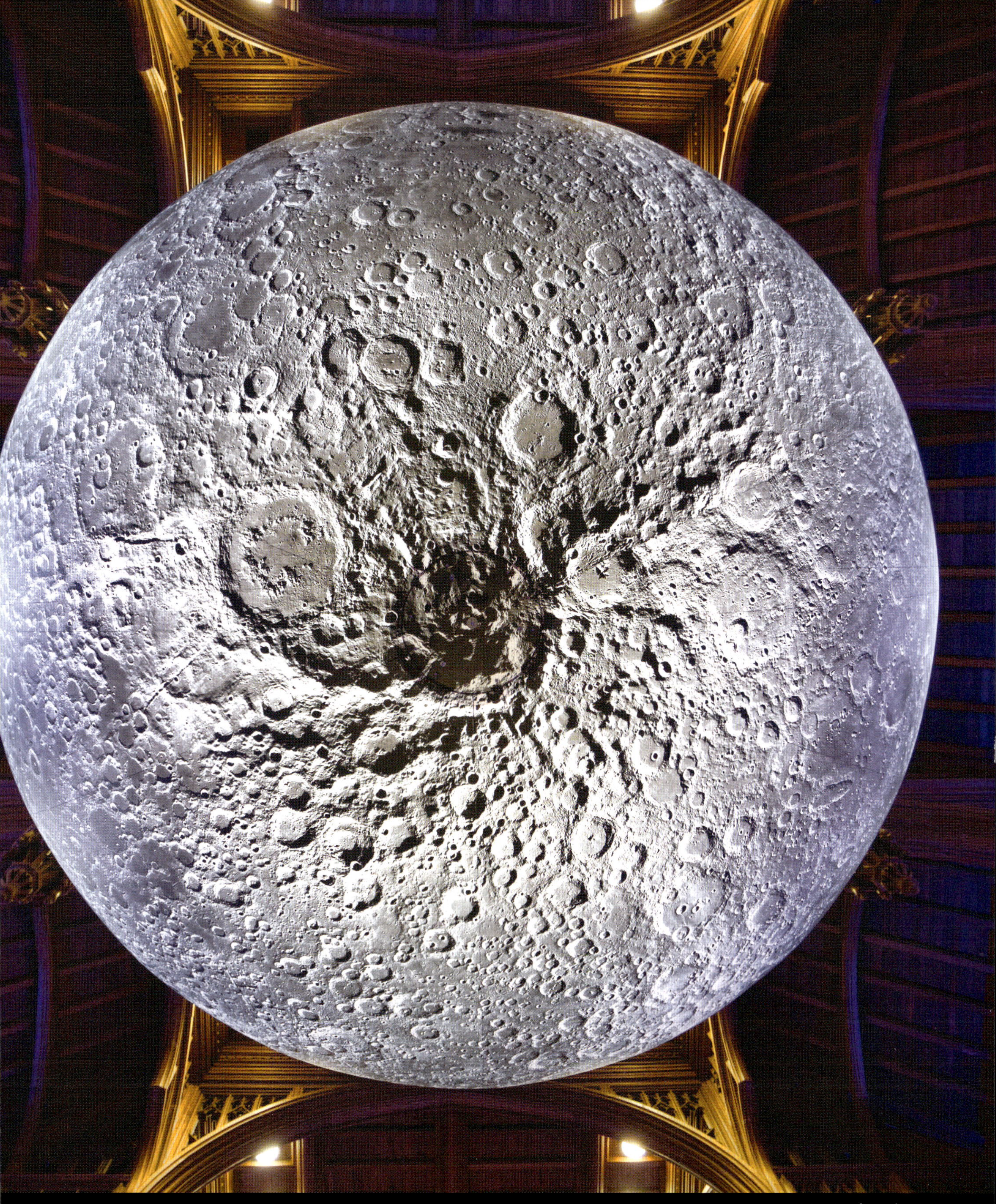

Gaia

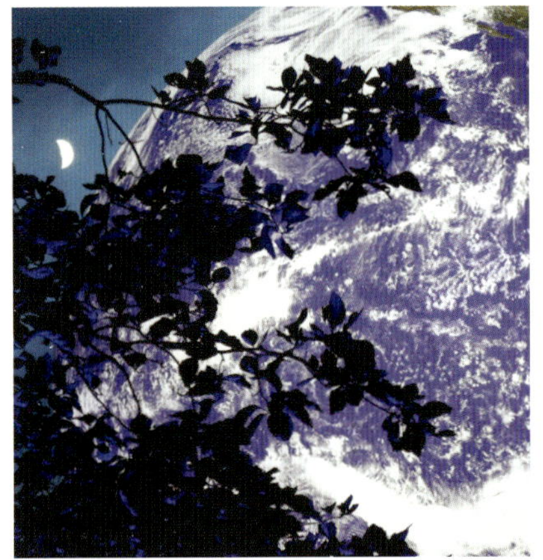

Bluedot Festival, Jodrell Bank, 2018

LJ: **We desperately need to change our habits to protect our planet. I hope Gaia enables people to see the Earth as a fragile and beautiful ecosystem.**

Developed as a comparative experience to *Museum of the Moon*, *Gaia* also measures seven metres in diameter, but features 120dpi detailed NASA imagery of Earth's surface, compiled from their Visible Earth series. The illuminated artwork provides the opportunity to see our planet on this scale, floating in three-dimensions.

A specially made surround-sound score by composer Dan Jones is played alongside the sculpture. As with *Museum of the Moon*, this is used to connect the surrounding architecture with the sculpture and creates an atmosphere that guides and informs the experience of the artwork.

The installation creates a sense of the 'overview effect', which was first described by author Frank White in 1987.[1] Common features of astronauts' experience of this include a feeling of awe for the planet, a profound understanding of the interconnection of all life, and a renewed sense of responsibility for taking care of the environment.

Over its lifetime, *Gaia* will be presented in a number of different ways, both indoors and outdoors. It will also act as a venue, with local hosts creating their own programme of events to take place beneath the artwork, including music, performance art, and space/environment-themed science events.

Unlike the Moon, which we have been gazing at for millennia, the first time humankind got to see Earth in its entirety as a blue marble floating in space was in 1972 with NASA's Apollo 17 mission. At that moment, our perception and understanding of our planet changed forever. Hanging in the black emptiness of space, Earth seemed isolated; a precious and fragile island of life.

Gaia was created in partnership with the Natural Environment Research Council (NERC), *Bluedot Festival* and the UK Association for Science and Discovery Centres.

1. Frank White, *The Overview Effect: Space Exploration and Human Evolution* (Boston: Houghton Mifflin Harcourt Publishing Company, 1987)

▶ *Bluedot Festival, Jodrell Bank, 2018*

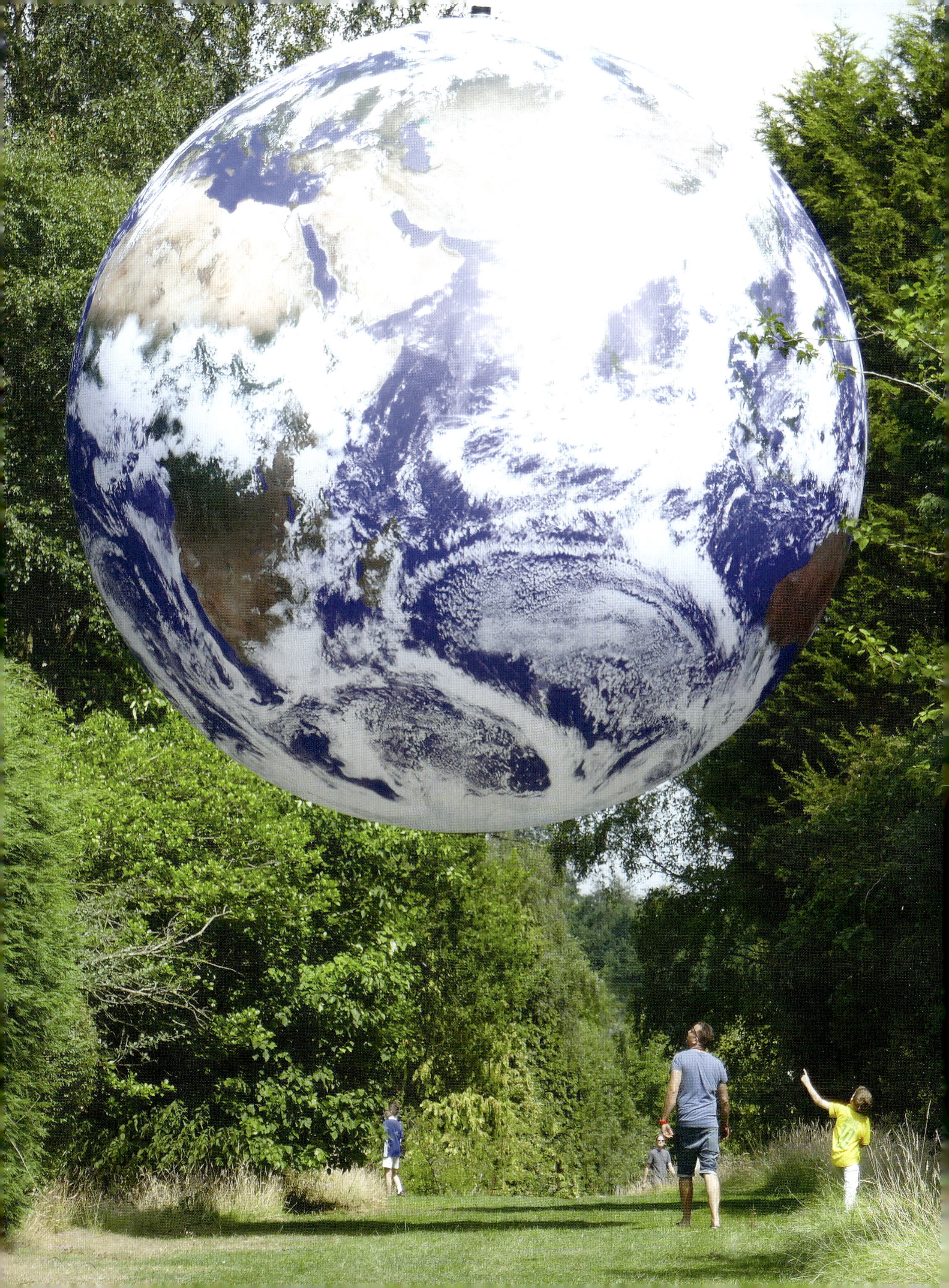

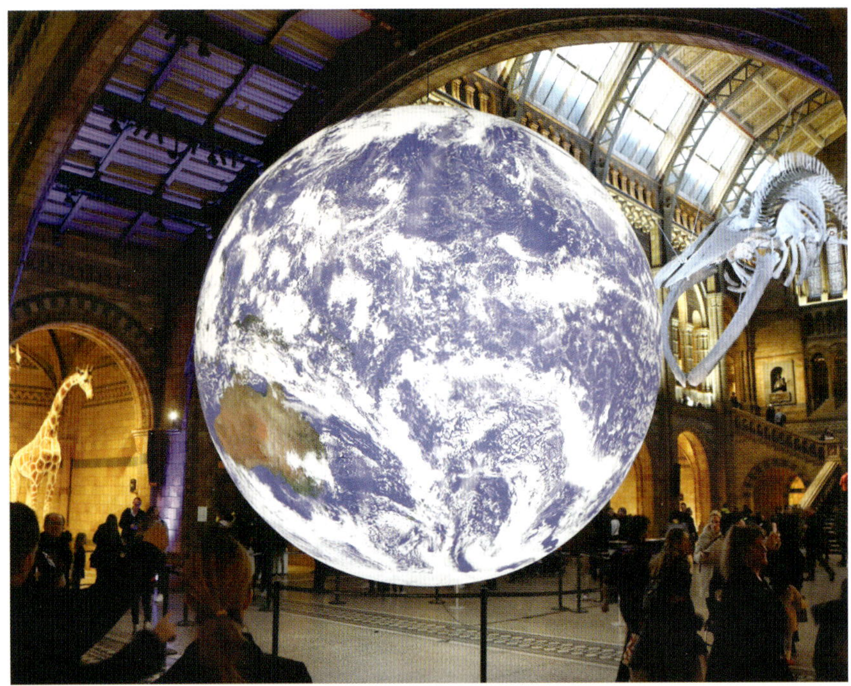

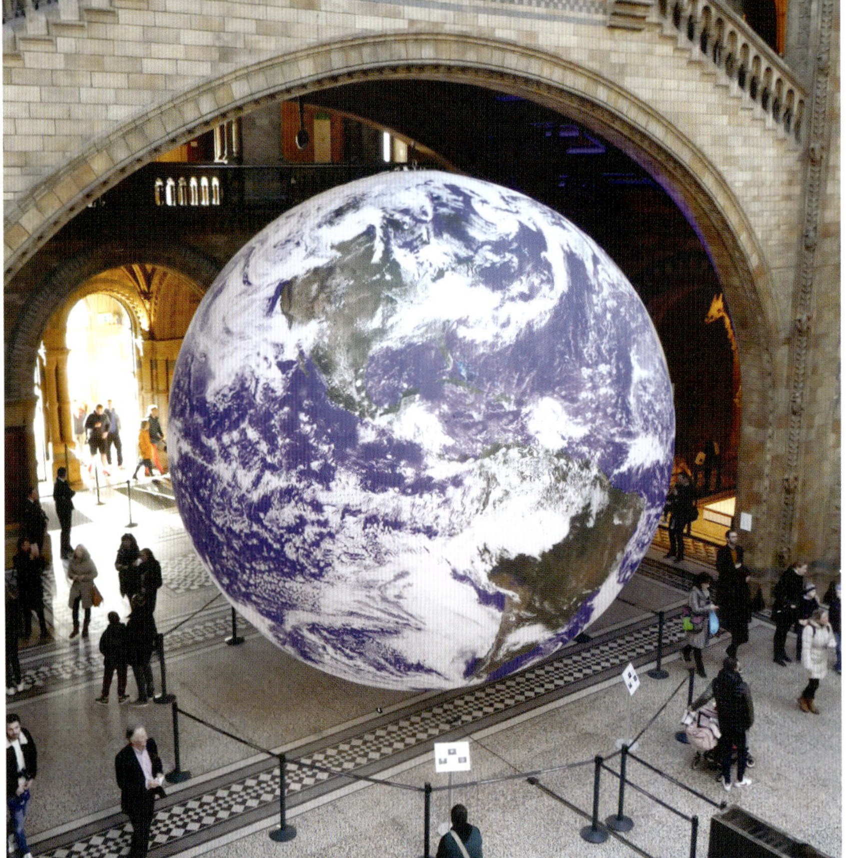

Natural History Museum, London, 2018

▶ *New Year Festival, Hsinchu, Taiwan, 2019*

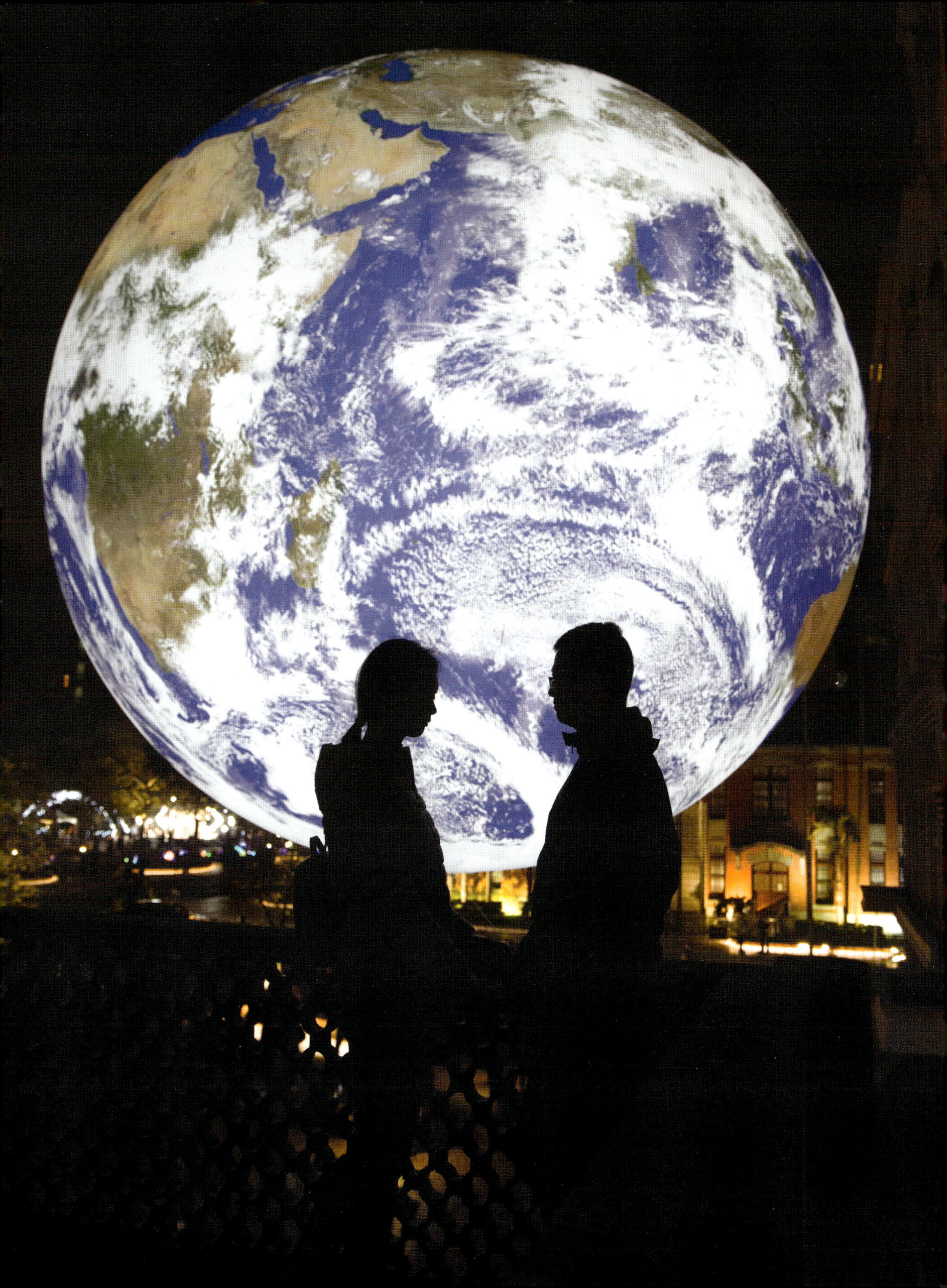

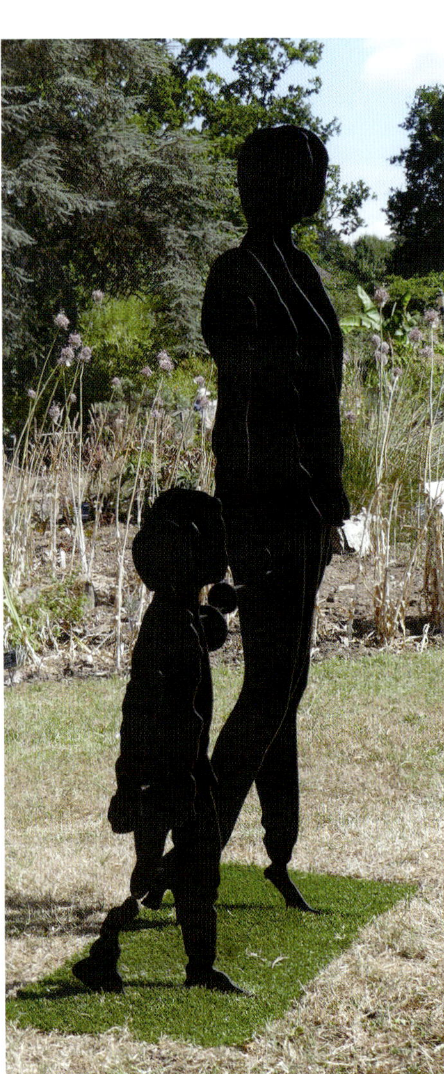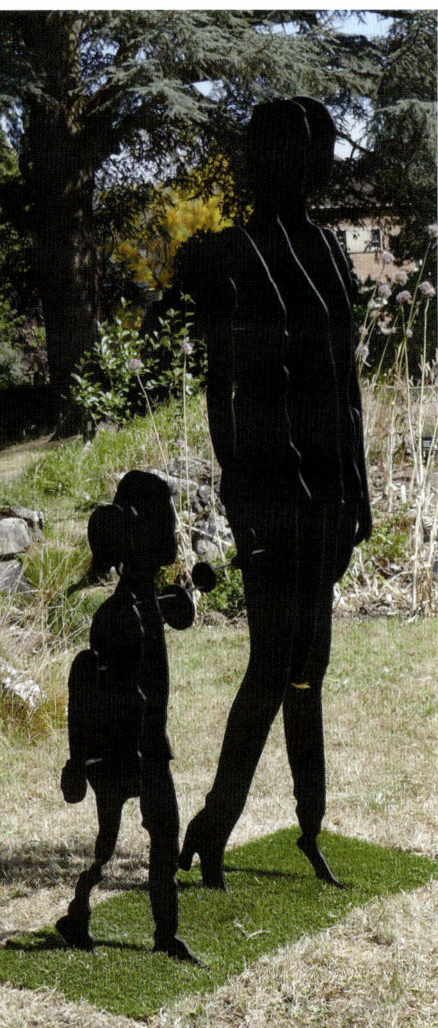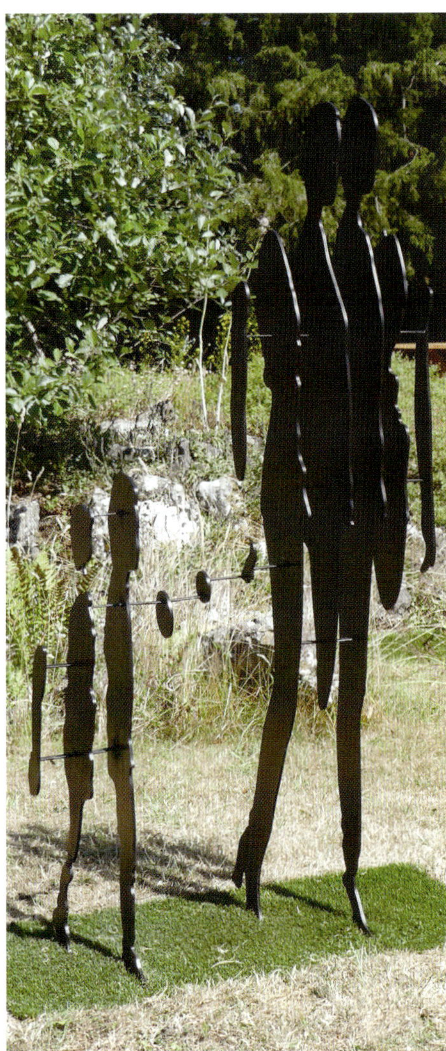

Impossible Garden: Mother and Child | University of Bristol Botanic Garden, 2018

'If the doors to perception were cleansed, then everything would appear to man as it is. Infinite.'

William Blake, *The Marriage of Heaven and Hell*, c.1790

Perception

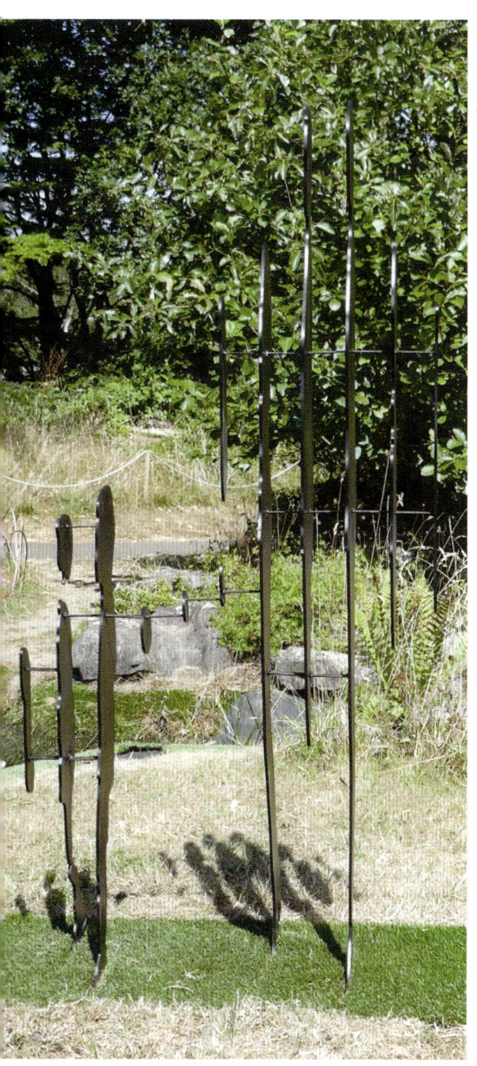

My red-green colour blindness has given me a natural interest in perception and the way we interpret the world around us. From an early age I've always known my vision and perception of things was a bit odd. I remember going hunting for strawberries in a local wood with my school and not finding a thing to eat. It was deeply frustrating. This slightly different, if not limited way of seeing things, could be one reason why I work as an artist. Our senses act like filters to the world and so I'm keen to explore the boundaries and limitations of this.

As part of *Impossible Garden*, a recent series of experimental sculptural works inspired by optical phenomena and developed in collaboration with Bristol Vision Institute, I displayed some glasses developed by an American company called Enchroma, which are designed to counter the effects of colour blindness. Specially invited colour blind guests tried on these glasses and were moved by the experience of seeing the landscape around them in a new way. As with my 'pixelated' sculpture *Maya*, which was installed within a busy train station, the journey of information between the object and mind of the viewer incited new ways of seeing and explored the edges of perception.

My interest in making visible and tangible that which is invisible and beyond our senses is a common theme, which has connected much of my work over the past two decades. One of my earliest artworks *Tide* attempted to render the invisible force of gravity both visible and audible through a live installation. While more recently, *Aeolus* made audible the surrounding winds through a network of vibrating strings attached to it. The *Kinetic Chandeliers* render the energy of the Sun both visible and audible through the shimmering display and quiet 'clinking' sounds of dozens of spinning glass radiometers.

Tōhoku Japanese Earthquake also visualises invisible forms and forces. Capturing this catastrophic natural disaster, the sculpture was made by taking the seismogram and rotating it, providing a new way of visualising data and documenting the event. This technique was used for a number of rotated data sculptures and also formed the basis of *Apollo* made seven years later.

Glass Microbiology came about through my interest in science communication, and realising that unlike the scientific imagery we receive through the media, viruses don't have colour. A tension arises between the beauty and intrigue of these forms and what they represent. *Inhale* is a recent artwork that also has a dark edge by enlarging harmful microscopic diesel soot particles in to a seemingly abstract sculptural form.

Tide

2001

Tide is based on Johannes Kepler's theories of the 'music of the spheres', the idea that the revolution of the planets generates a celestial harmony of profound beauty, and references early scientific apparatus, as studied in the Science Museum, London. The artwork functions as both an astronomical clock and a media art exhibit.

As the Earth and Moon move through space and time around the Sun, our position also changes within this shifting triangle of spheres. Tide is a live installation controlled by this changing spatial relationship. A gravity meter measures Earth's tide, caused by the changing gravitational pull of the Moon and Sun upon it. This information is represented as a video projection showing a full 24 hours of altering gravity. Through the use of water pumps, the received data is also made to control water levels within each sculptural object. A friction device makes the glass of each sculpture resonate and sing (like rubbing a finger around the rim of a wine glass). The rise and fall of water levels over time, from high to low tide, changes the note produced by each singing sculpture.

These machines alter their state with the live change in the altering positions of the Moon and Sun in relation to the installation. Two years of extensive research was carried out in the development of the work. Advice and support came from over a hundred individuals and organisations from around the world, including the University of Hawaii Astronomy Department, medieval musicologists, dark sky campaigners, and a seventeenth-century glass harmonica maker. NASA provided information on their three-dimensional gravity meter used in submarines for stealth navigation.

Funded by the Institute of Physics and Arts Council England, Tide was commissioned by DA2. Engineers and glassblowers from the University of Bristol built the sculptural elements of the work.

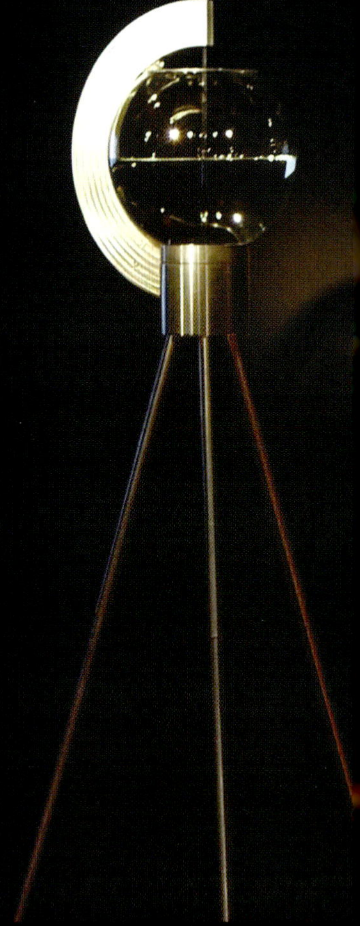

LJ: *The idea for Tide came from living in Bristol, where we have the second highest tidal range in the world; there's a 13-metre gap between high and low tide. Every day I would cycle to work over the River Avon and notice this huge variation.*

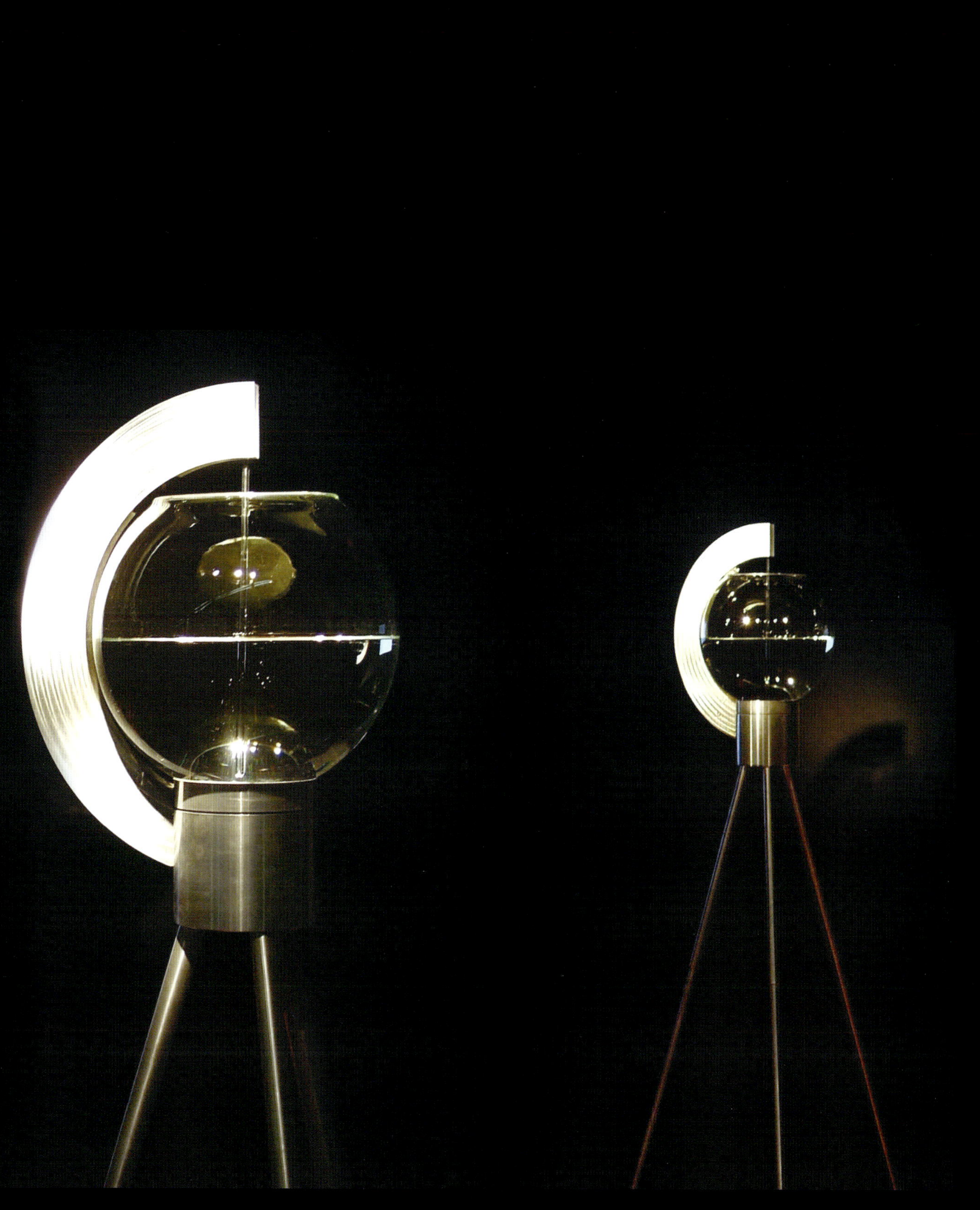

Aeolus

2011–2012

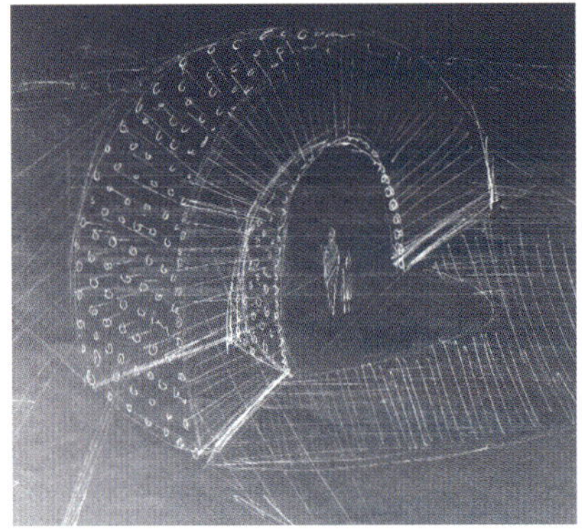

Sketch for Aeolus

LJ: Aeolus *was inspired by a research trip to Iran in 2007 where I explored the mosques of Isfahan and also interviewed a Qanat desert well digger about his life. He spoke of the wells singing in the wind which led me to think about the acoustics of architecture.*

Aeolus, named after the ruler of the four winds in Greek mythology, is both a giant stringed musical instrument and an acoustic and optical pavilion, designed to make audible the silent shifting patterns of the wind and to visually amplify the ever-changing sky.

Without any electrical power, *Aeolus* sonifies the wind using a web of Aeolian harp strings attached to some of the sculpture's steel tubes. Like cats' whiskers, sensitive to the slightest touch, the strings vibrate and sing in the wind. The tubes are tuned to an Aeolian scale, and even on a still day hum at a series of low frequencies.

Beneath the arch a viewer can look out through 310 mirrored, steel tubes. These 'light pipes' act to frame, invert and magnify the landscape around the pavilion, changing minute by minute as the clouds move across the sky.

Aeolus took over three years to complete, during which time Luke created over 400 drawings to communicate his ideas to colleagues. Dozens of people were brought together to provide their expertise, including art managers, sound engineers, structural engineers, computer-aided designers, steel manufacturers, fabricators and welders.

Aeolus is the result of a collaboration between Luke, the Institute of Sound and Vibration Research at the University of Southampton, and the Acoustics Research Centre at the University of Salford. *Aeolus* toured in the UK to Canary Wharf, London; Lyme Park, Cheshire; MediaCityUK, Salford, and the Eden Project, Cornwall. It is now installed permanently at the production site of Airbus, a leading aircraft manufacturer based in Bristol.

▶ *Lyme Park, Cheshire, 2011*

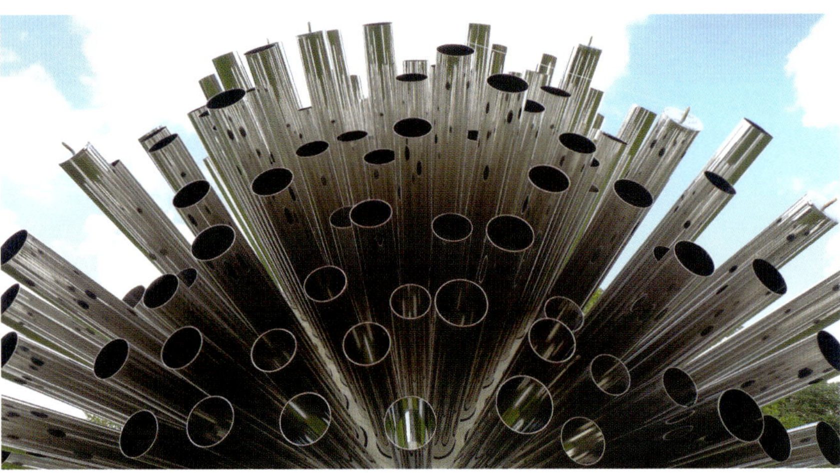

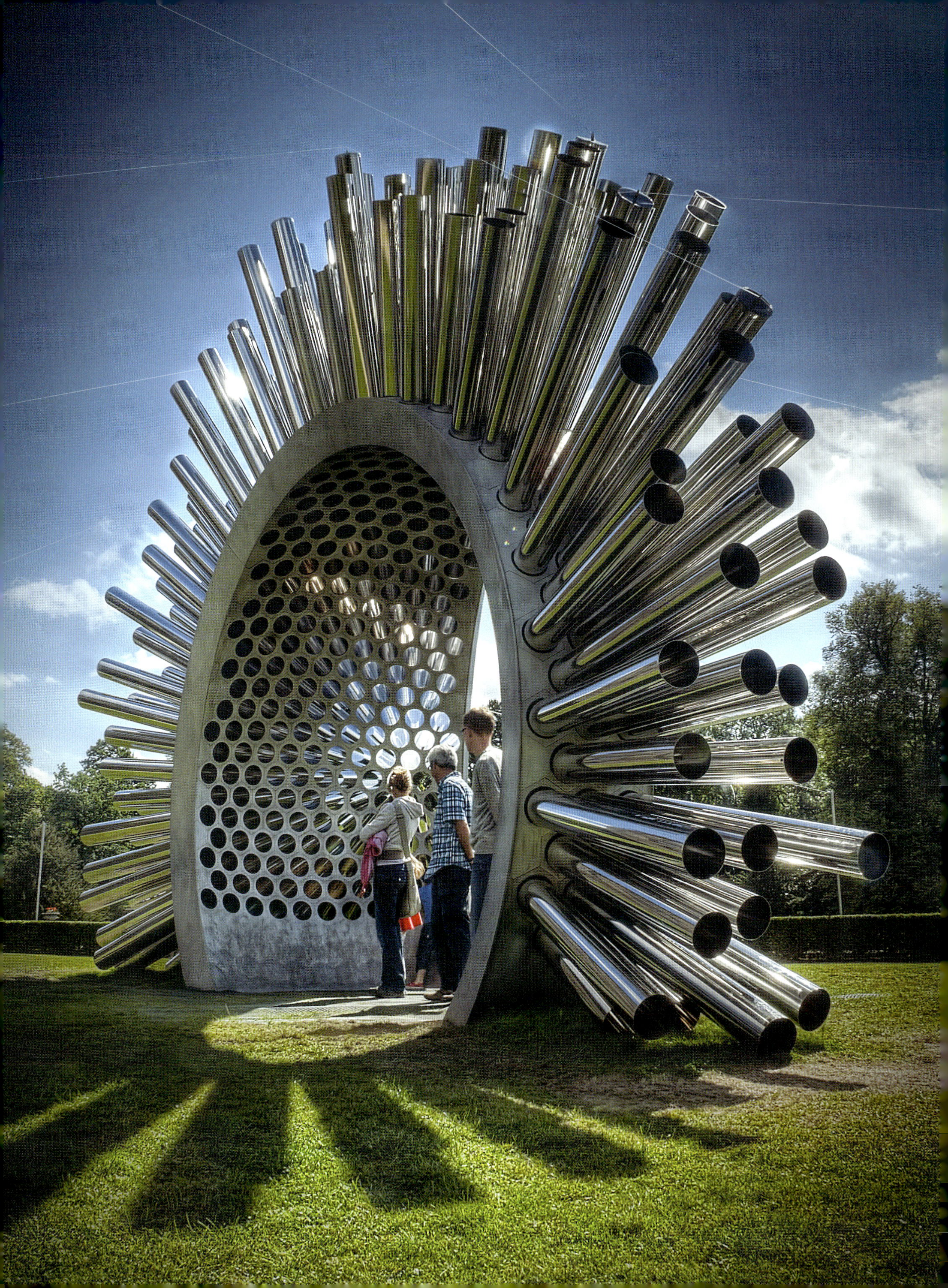

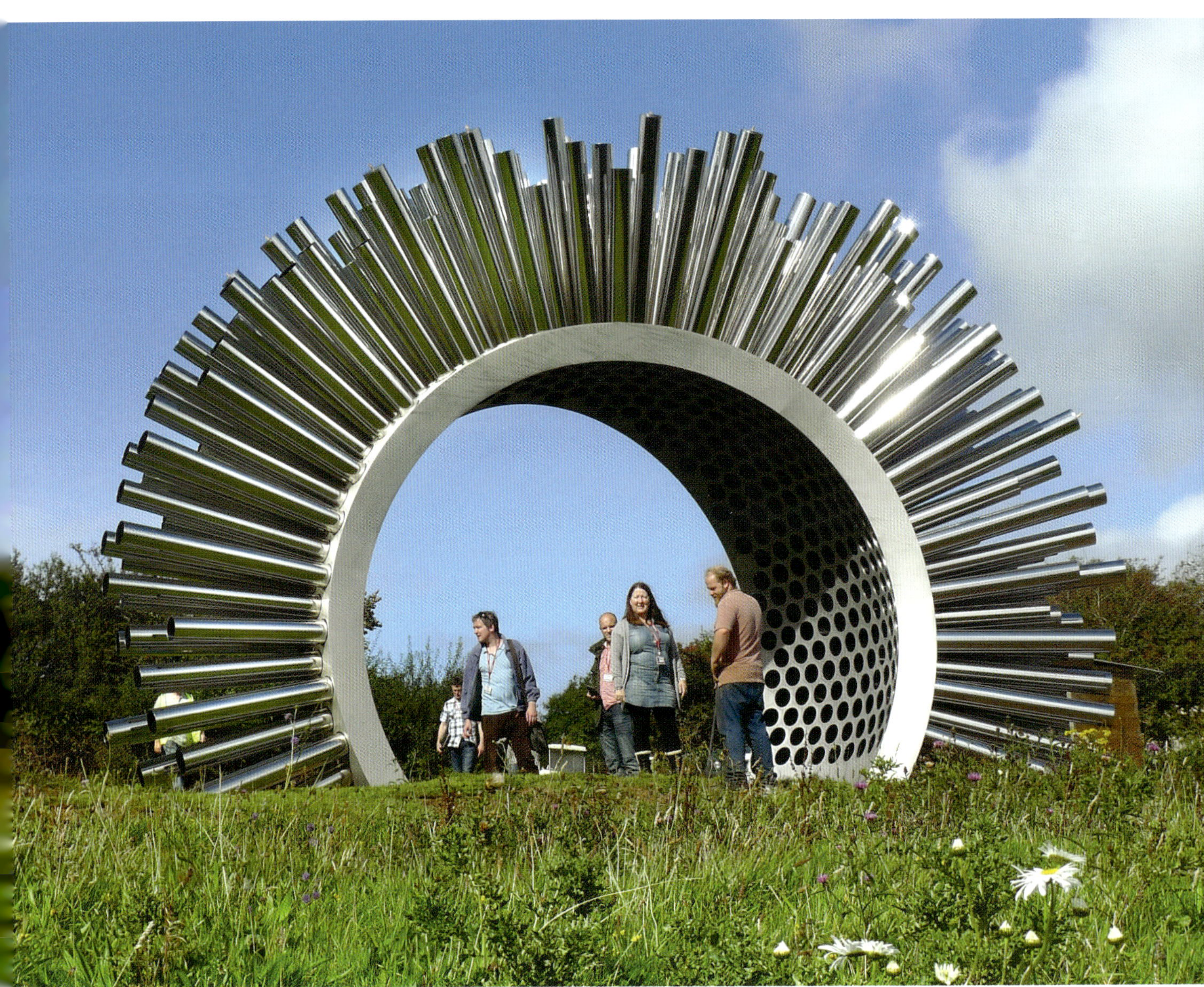

Eden Project, 2011

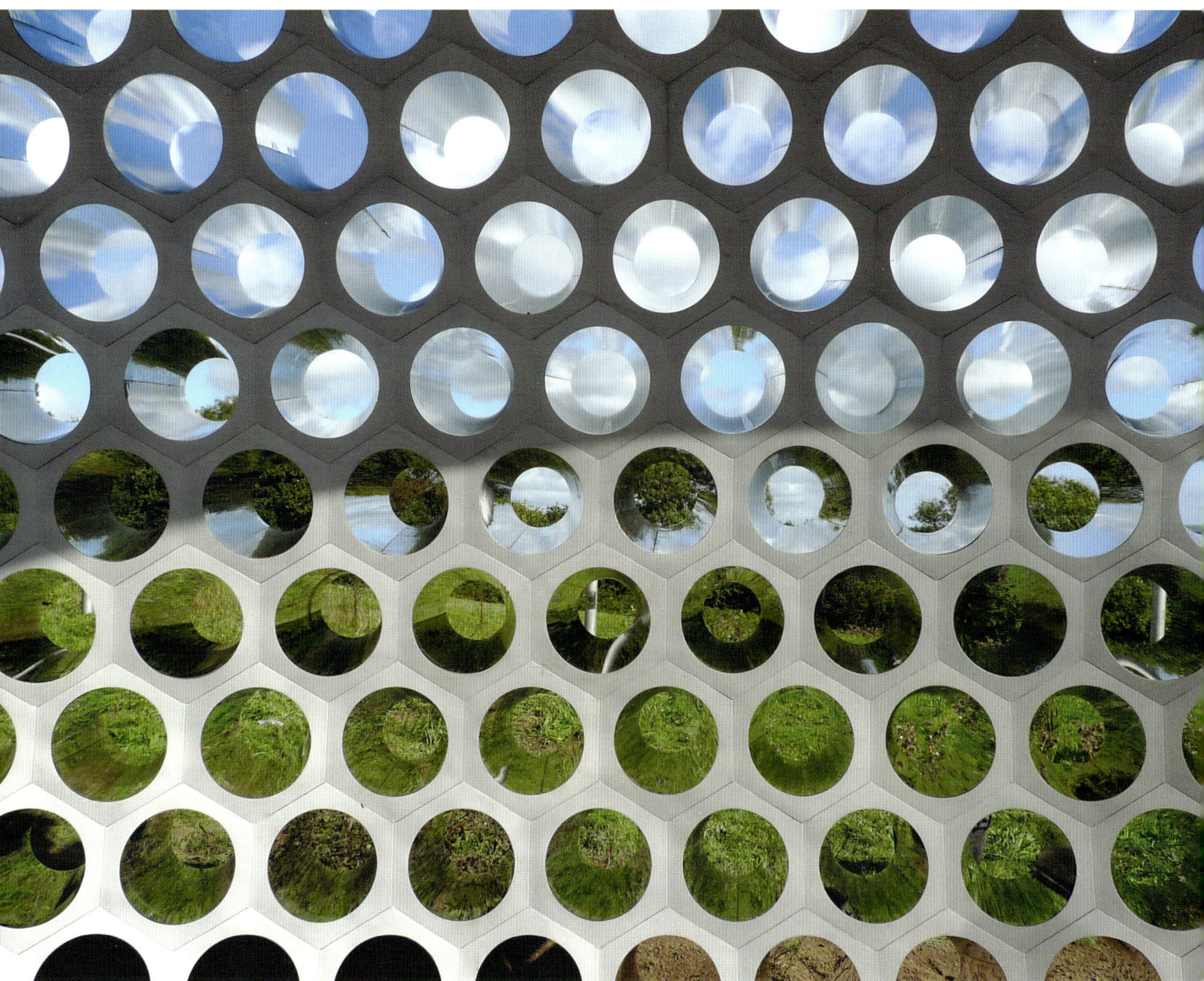

Kinetic Chandeliers

2012–2014

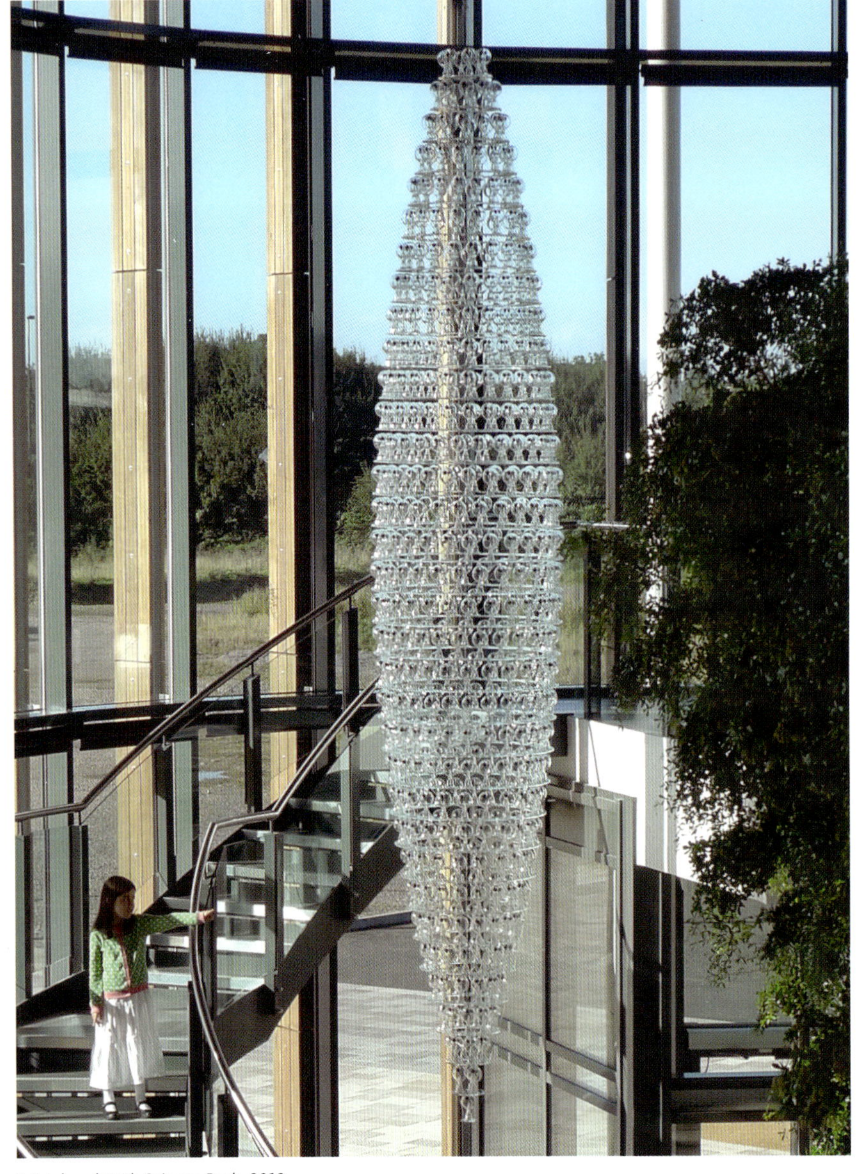

Bristol and Bath Science Park, 2012

These solar powered *Kinetic Chandeliers* consist of dozens of glass radiometers, which shimmer and flicker as they turn in the sunlight. Altering their speed with the subtle changes in lighting conditions, the vanes of each radiometer speed up and slow down throughout the day.

Beautiful shadows are formed as sunlight passes through the tiers of glass. Usually only experienced as a tactile sensation, the energy of the Sun is rendered both visible and audible through the chandeliers' shimmering display and a quiet 'clinking' sound.

Historically, chandeliers have been made from glass due to the light-scattering abilities of crystal, which brighten up a dark space. The *Kinetic Chandeliers* turn that original function inward and instead absorb light from the Sun through a mechanism that makes us aware of its power in unexpected ways.

The largest *Kinetic Chandelier*, commissioned for Bristol and Bath Science Park, is 17 feet tall and contains 665 radiometers. Chandeliers have also been commissioned for Chrysler Museum of Art, USA and National Glass Centre, UK. They have been temporarily presented at Museum of Art and Design, New York; Weizmann Institute, Tel Aviv; Des Moines Arts Centre, USA and National Centre for Craft and Design, UK.

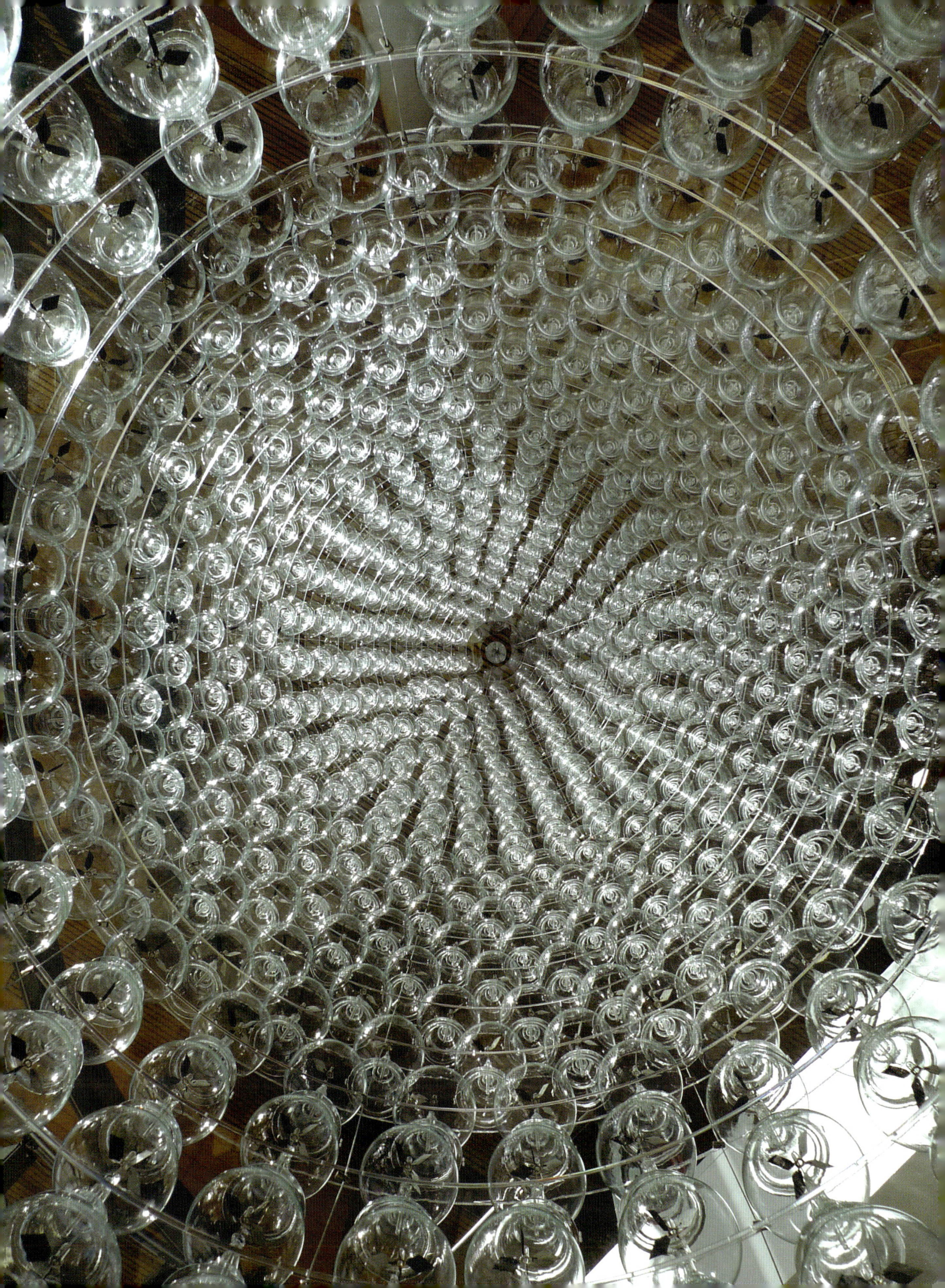

Glass Microbiology
since 2004

Glass Microbiology is an ongoing body of glass sculptures. Made to contemplate the global impact of each disease, the artworks are representations of viruses and have been created as an alternative to the artificially coloured imagery received through the media. In fact, viruses have no colour as they are smaller than the wavelength of light. By extracting the colour from the imagery and creating beautiful jewel-like sculptures in glass, a complex tension arises between the artworks' beauty and what they represent. Photographs of the artworks are even used in medical journals and the media as useful representations of virology within the scientific community.

The sculptures are approximately one million times larger than the actual viruses depicted, and are designed in consultation with virologists using a combination of scientific photographs and models. They are made in collaboration with glassblowers Brian Jones and Norman Veitch.

The first *Glass Microbiology* sculpture, made in 2004, was of the HIV virus. This was originally made as something that could be held, to contemplate the global impact of the virus.

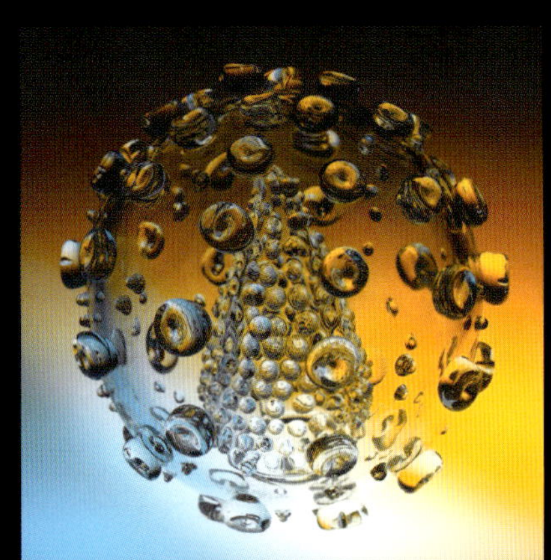

HIV | *2004*

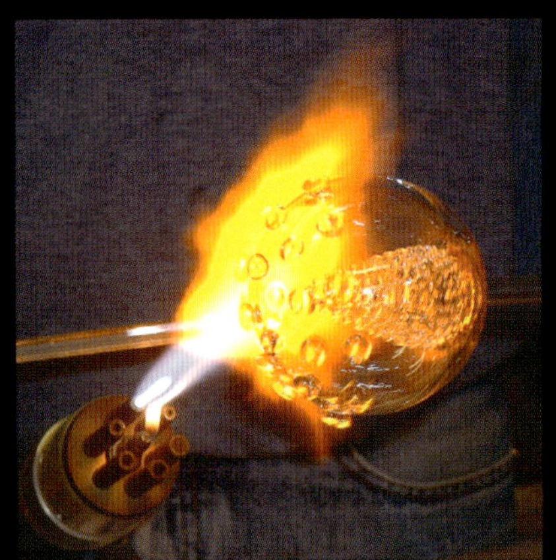

Making of HIV

The sculptures are in private and public collections around the world, including the Metropolitan Museum of Art, New York; European Museum of Modern Glass, Germany; Natural History Museum, Kuwait and the Museum of Glass, Washington, USA.

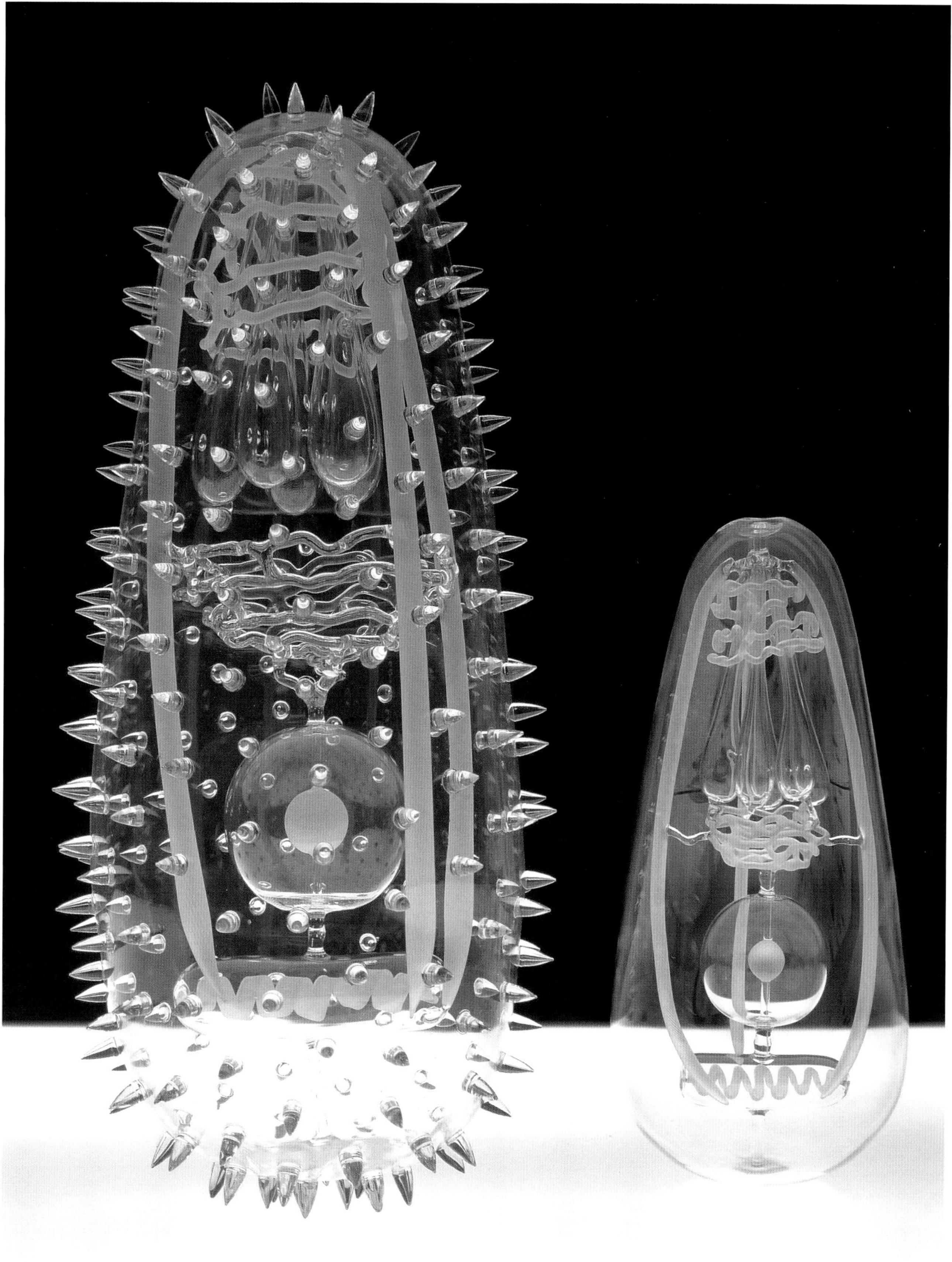

Malaria with and without spikes | 2010

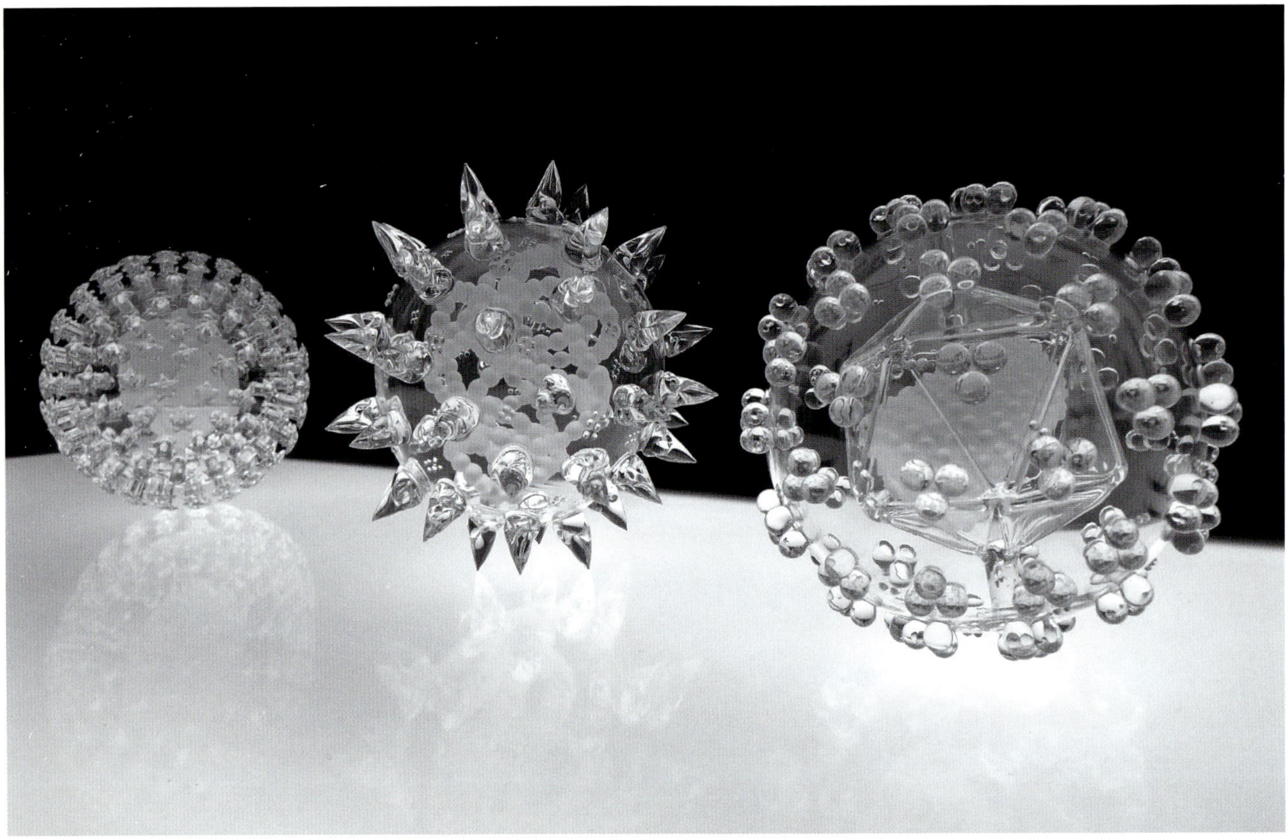

Papillomavirus, **Untitled Future Mutation** *and* **HIV** | *2011*

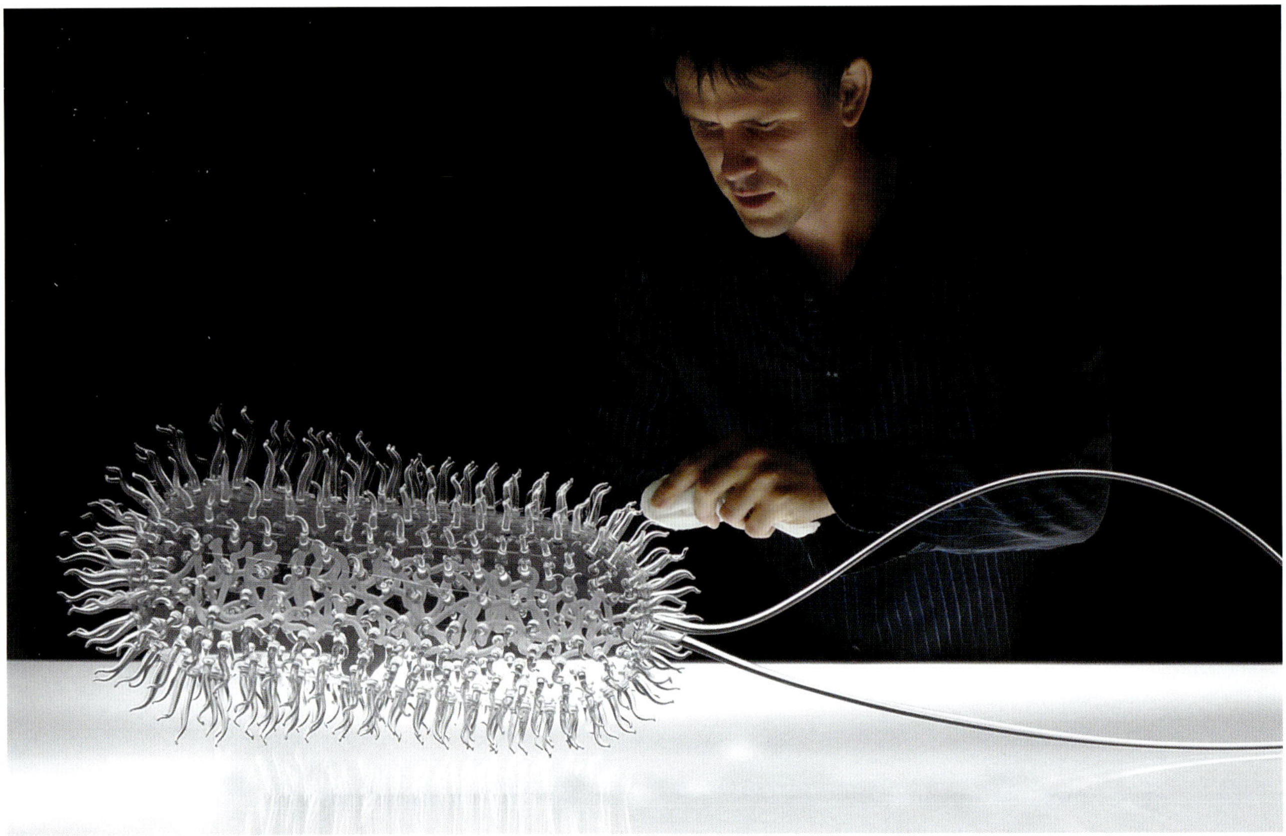

E. coli | *2010*

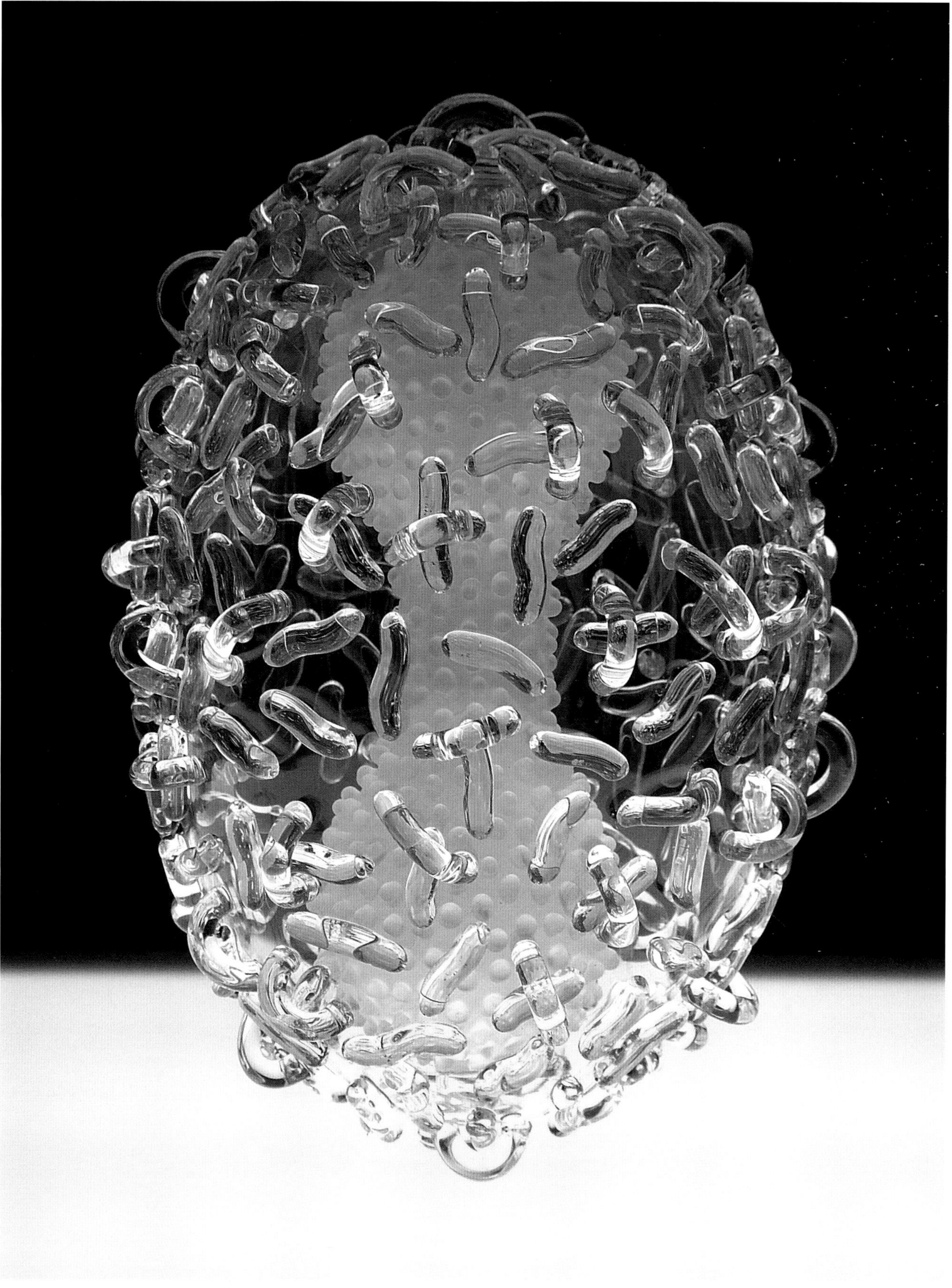

Smallpox | 2008

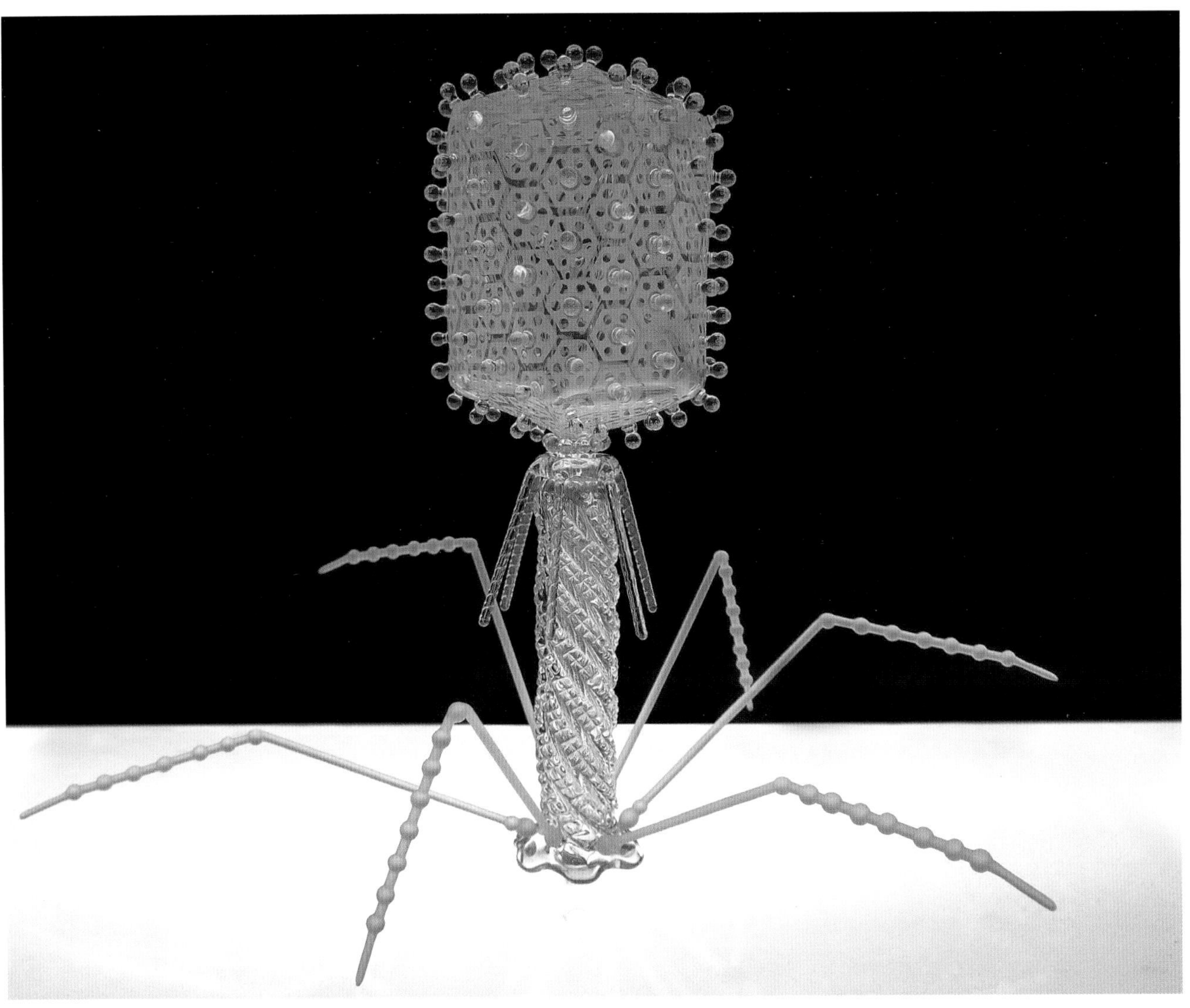

T4 Bacteriophage | 2011

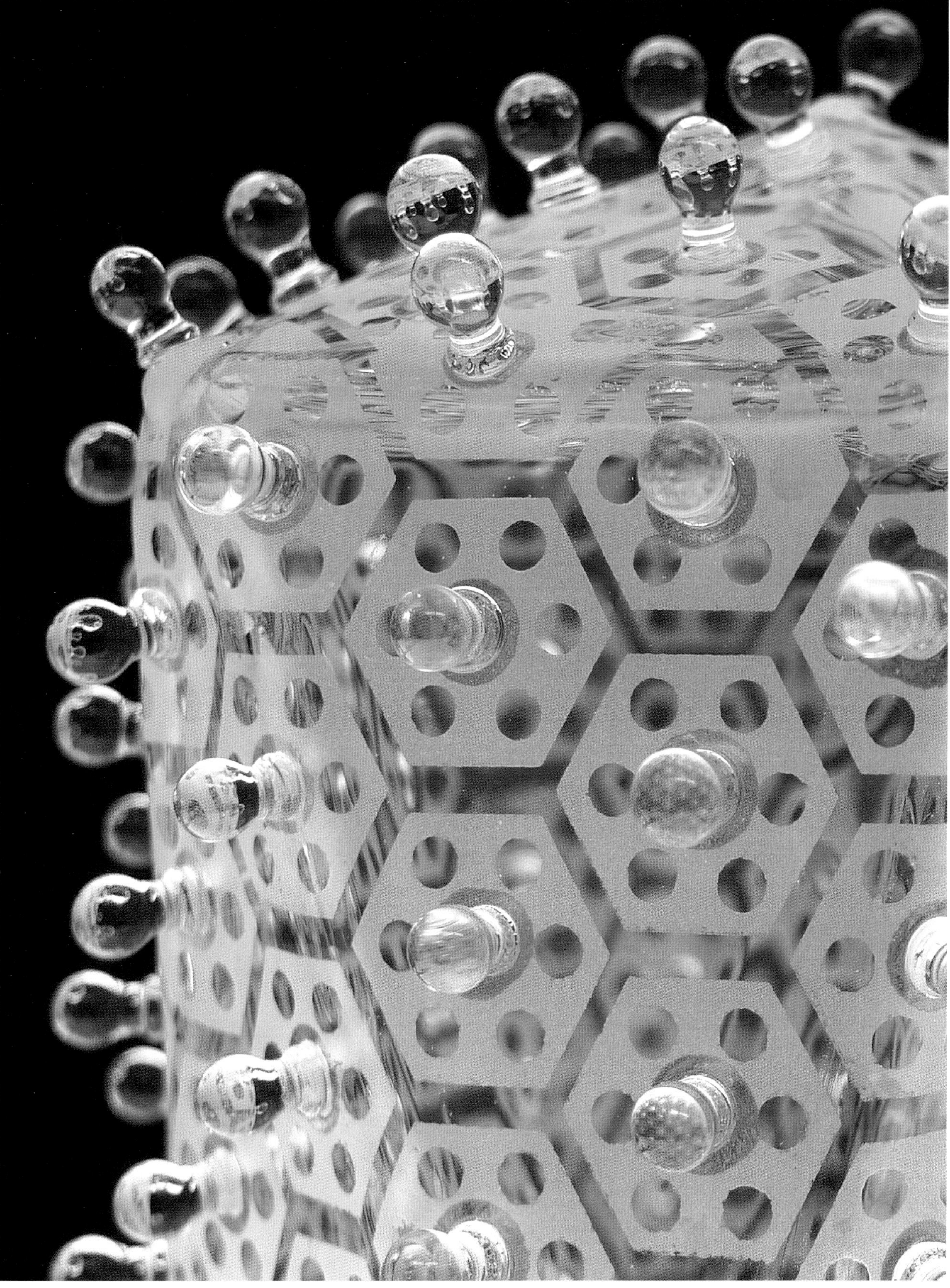

T4 Bacteriophage detail

E. coli

2015

At 90 feet long, *E. coli* is five million times bigger than the real bacterium and makes the microscopic world around us visible. Standing underneath the vast inflatable bacterium alters our personal sense of scale. Created as an experimental object for contemplation, the sculpture can look scary, alien, even comical.

The artwork was also made to encourage us to reflect upon the importance of bacteria in our lives. There are around ten times more bacterial cells on and within our bodies than there are human cells. Although some forms of Escherichia coli (E. coli) bacteria can cause illness and even death in humans, the use of the bacteria is also vital in medical research.

E. coli was commissioned by The University of Sheffield for *KrebsFest*, and has since been presented in other venues around the UK, including the Eden Project, Cornwall and Oxford University Museum of Natural History.

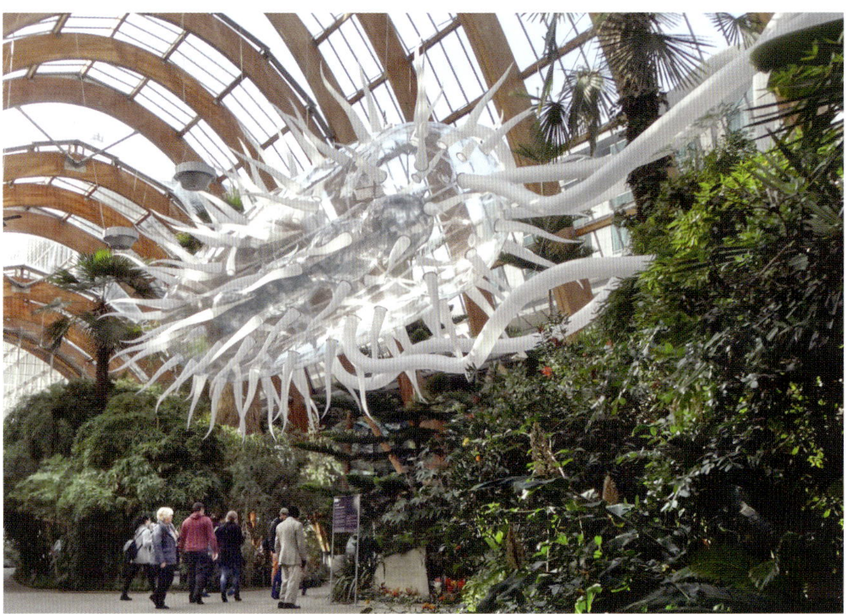

KrebsFest, The University of Sheffield, 2015

LJ: *Bacteria were the earliest form of life on our planet and as such the artwork could be considered a curious portrait of our distant ancestors. If there is life on other planets (or moons) in our solar system, it is likely it will look like this.*

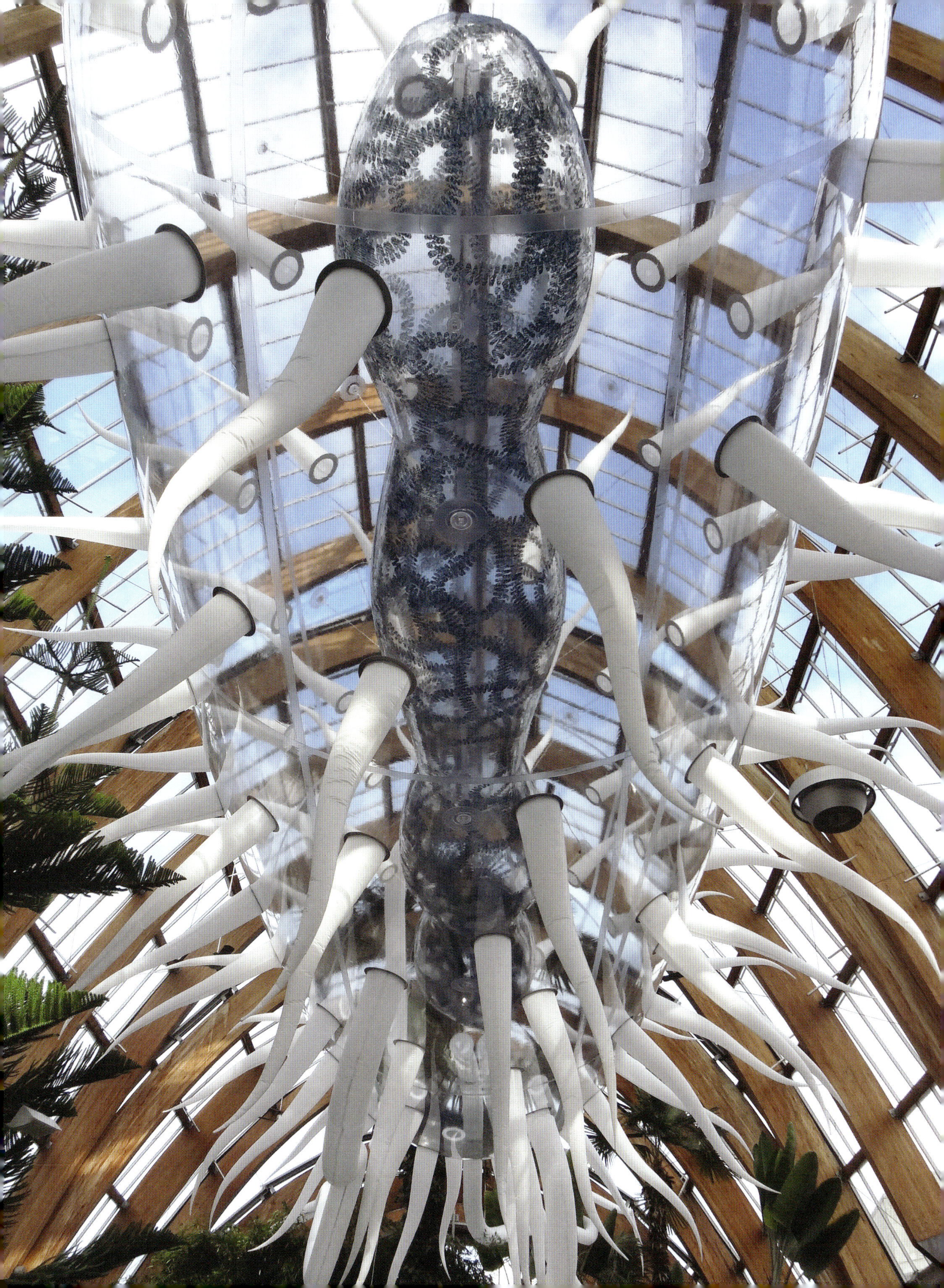

Tōhoku Japanese Earthquake
2011

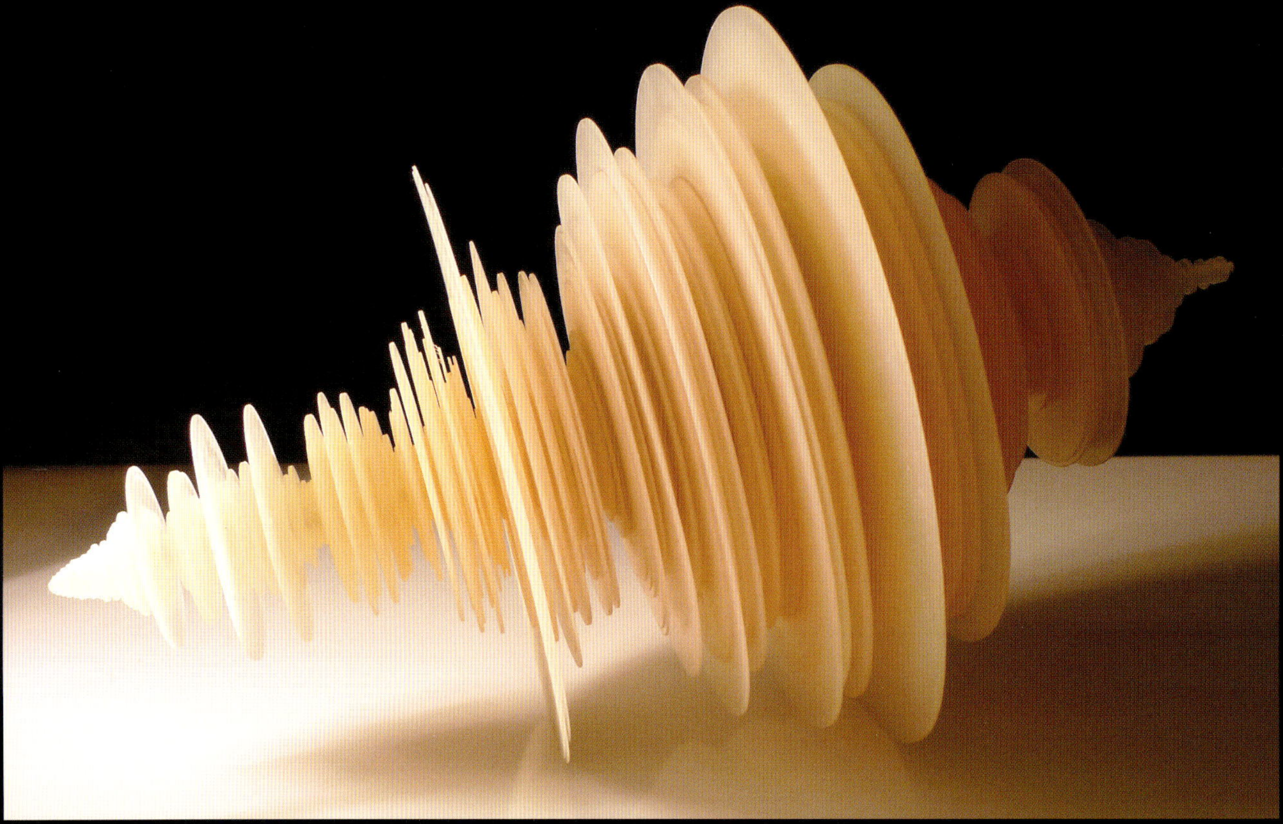

This sculpture was made to contemplate the 2011 Tōhoku earthquake and subsequent tsunami in Japan. To create it, a seismogram of the earthquake was rotated using computer-aided design and then printed in three-dimensions using rapid prototyping technology. The sculpture represents nine minutes of the earthquake.

The artwork is one of a series of rotated data sculptures exploring how data is read and can be represented and interpreted.

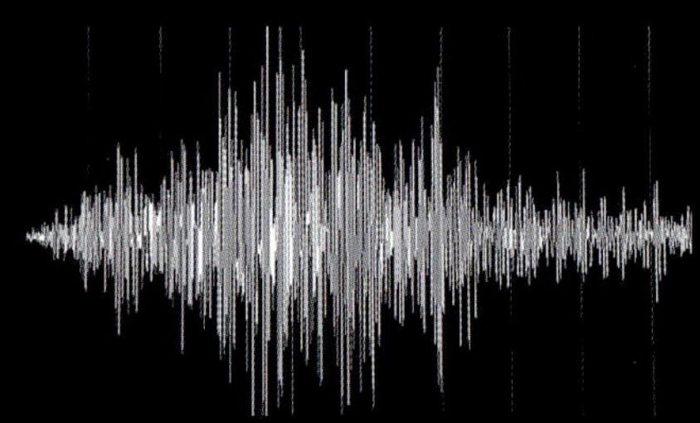

Nine-minute seismogram of the 2011 Tōhoku earthquake

Apollo

2018

Apollo was made by taking a sound file from a section of music, *Etude No. 2* by musician Philip Glass, and rotating it about its axis to create the form. Representing the first ten seconds of the music, the sound-wave sculpture (named after the Greek god of music) consists of approximately 80 hand-blown coloured glass roundels fused together. Like Luke's other rotated data sculptures, invisible sound waves were rotated, solidified and turned to glass.

Apollo was commissioned to help fund-raise for a new extension at St George's; a world-class concert hall in Bristol, which celebrates music in all its forms. The selected music is especially fitting as Philip Glass performed it at his first visit to St George's in 2013. The 3.62 metre-tall sculpture is suspended in the foyer of their new building.

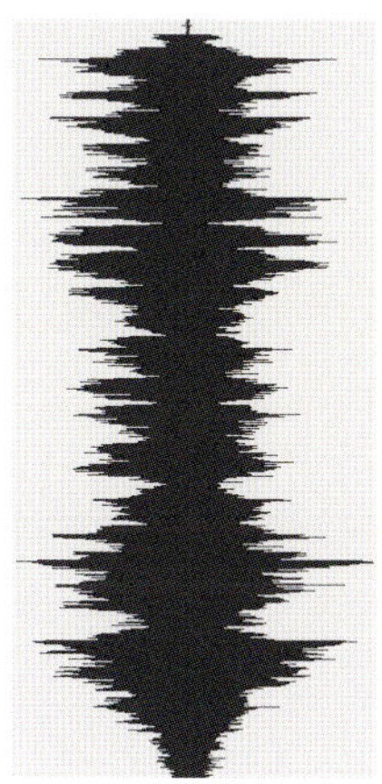

Ten seconds of the sound wave from Etude No.2 *by Philip Glass*

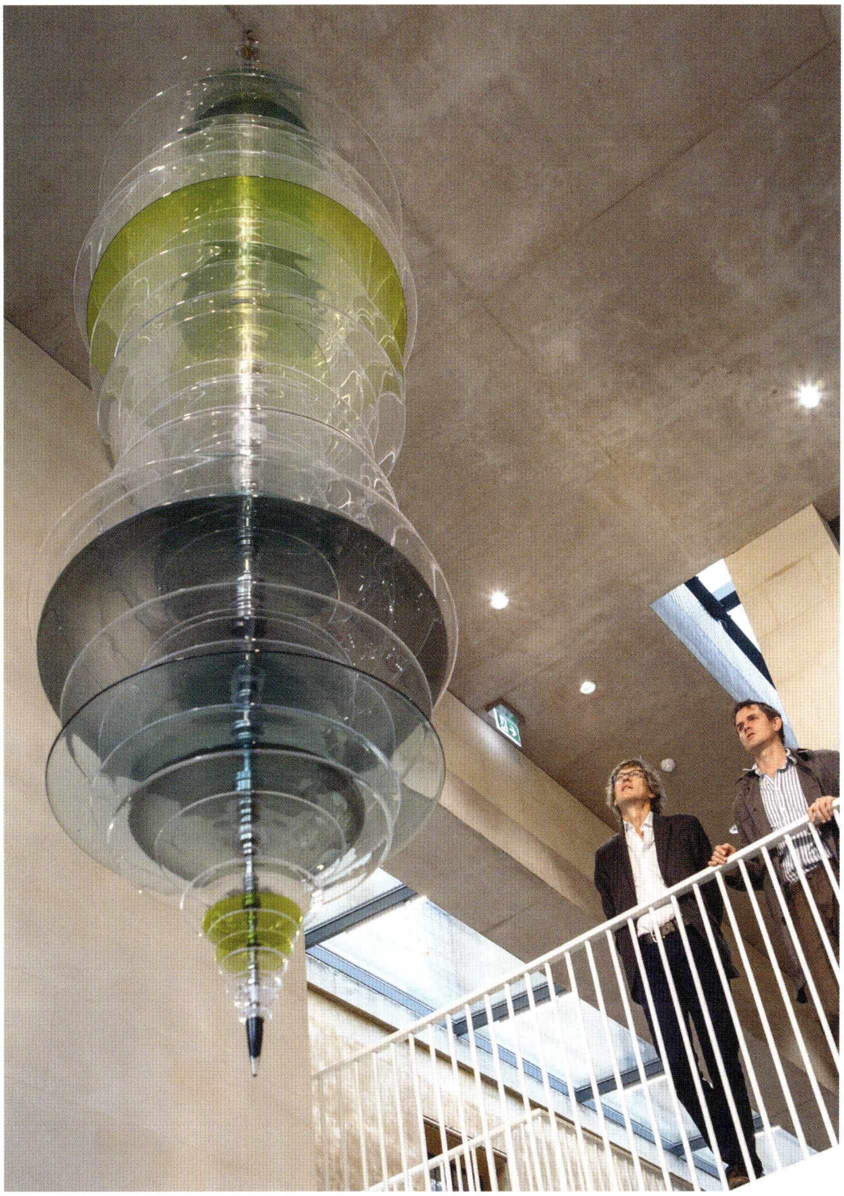

Maya

2013

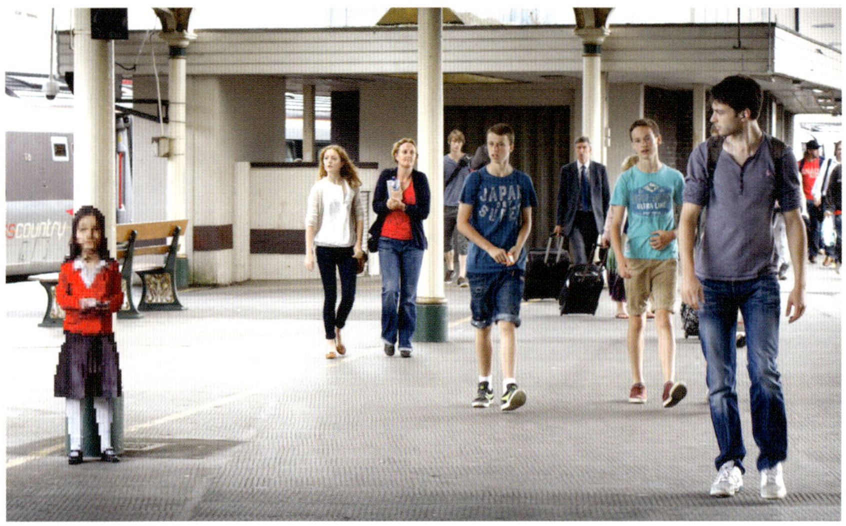

Maya is a sculpture which acts as a three-dimensional pixelated portrait of Luke's daughter. As with a heavily pixelated two-dimensional image made of squares, from a distance the sculpture can be easily read; however, as the viewer gets closer the object appears to fragment into cubes.

Maya was installed at Bristol Temple Meads train station in the UK. During the day, when large numbers of people were around, she blended into the crowd. At night, she looked out of place. A train was even delayed when its driver mistakenly thought he saw a vulnerable schoolgirl standing at the end of the platform.

To make the artwork, Maya was 3D scanned using an Xbox Kinect. The body scan was pixelated into cubes known as voxels, and then the model was created from precisely cut sheets of aluminium. Over 5,000 small 12 millimetre-square coloured stickers were printed and painstakingly fixed on to the surface. Printing was completed at the Centre for Fine Print Research (CFPR), University of West of England, Bristol, where Luke was a Senior Research Fellow.

Maya was part of Bristol Temple Quarter commissions coordinated by Watershed, Knowle West Media Centre and MAYK, with support from Bristol City Council and Arts Council England.

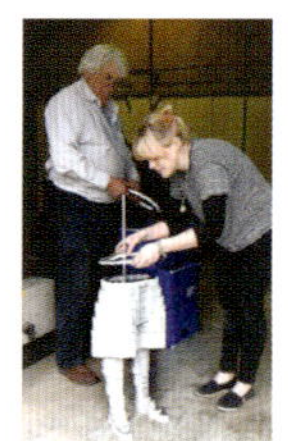 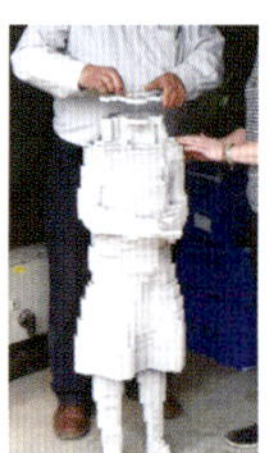 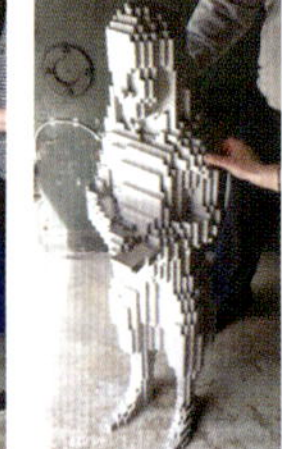

Constructing Maya

LJ: *From the age of three my daughter, Maya, could use an iPhone. For her, the technology was like a pencil, just another everyday tool. The artwork was in part inspired by my concern for her growing up in the digital age.*

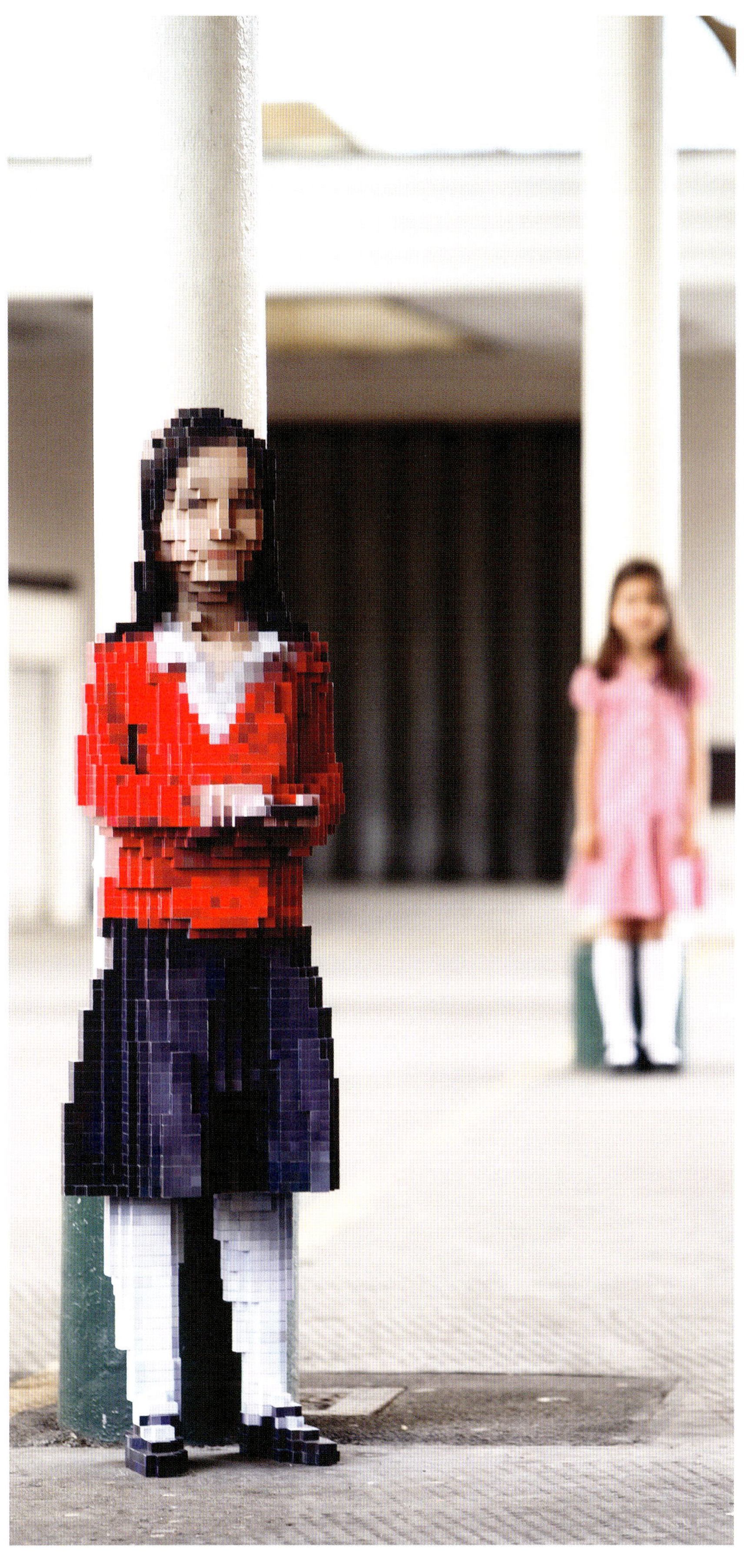

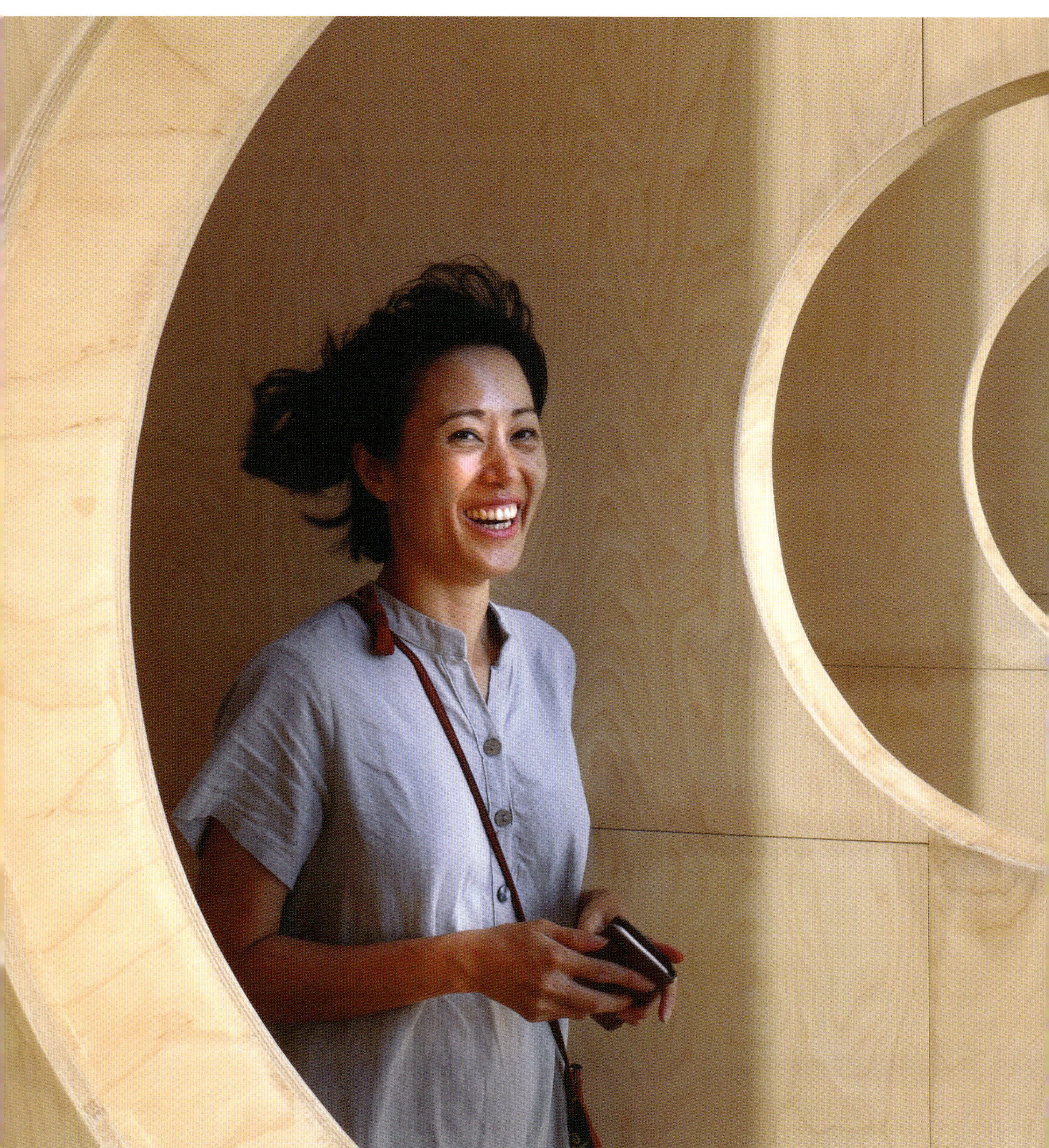

Han River Pavilion | *Seoul, South Korea, 2018*

Place

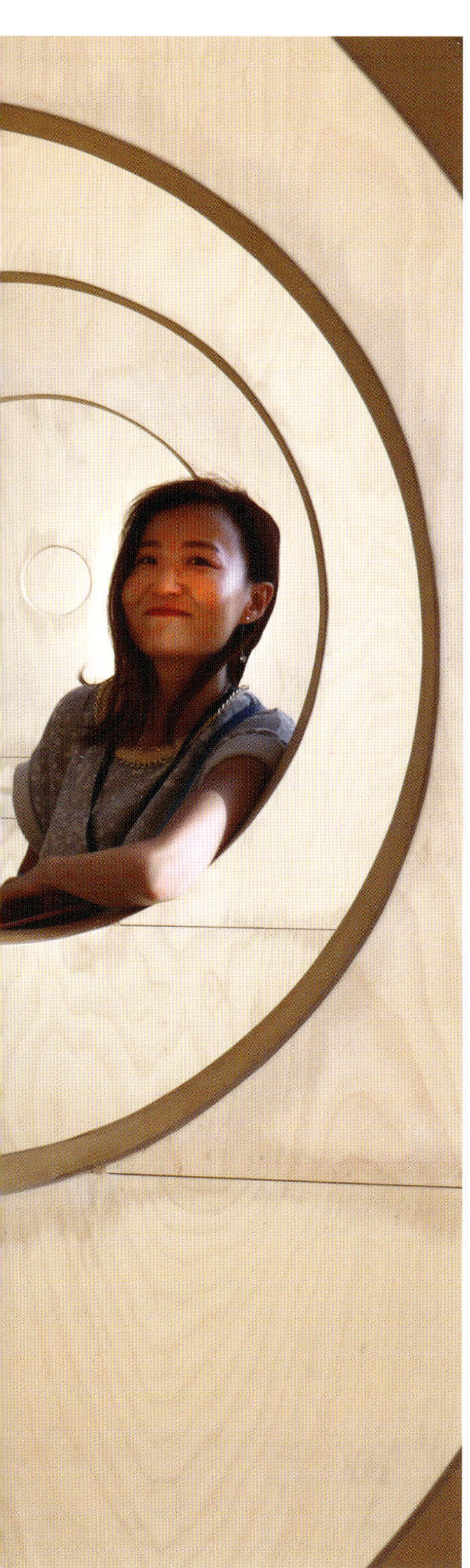

I often get approached by organisations that want to commission me to make an artwork for a specific place; whether it is a town/city, or a particular building or community. Considering what and whom the artwork is for is a priority.

Permanent public art which is created in response to a specific place or location can be incredibly problematic and difficult to create successfully. Often artworks are chosen by a risk-averse committee of stakeholders all arriving with their own agendas. The artworks may be required to last 20 years or more, with little or no plan and budget for maintenance put in place. They are required to be weather-proof, vandal-resistant and pass rigorous health and safety assessments. The artist's original intentions can get lost through processes of value engineering, and genuine public engagement can be difficult to achieve. As such, I'm drawn more to making temporary public artworks as they provide greater freedom to experiment and take risks. Budgets are generally smaller, but there is less pressure and fewer restrictions. A good temporary public artwork will exceed the expectations of the commissioners and lead to all sorts of unexpected positive outcomes.

Treasured City was made to animate the UK town of Scunthorpe, celebrating its history and culture, while also bringing more visitors to the arts centre which commissioned the project. As a kind of creative treasure hunt which took place across the city, it was wonderful to see so many local people excited about getting involved; many of whom had never visited the arts centre before. Likewise, *My RSC Gallery* was an exhibition full of artworks made by local residents and theatre staff of the Royal Shakespeare Theatre in Stratford-upon-Avon when it was being built. Directly involving the people who were impacted by the theatre helped to promote a sense of ownership.

As well as this notion of placemaking – prompting people to think again and reimagine the places they occupy – many of my projects draw directly from architecture, design and engineering to become places in their own right. *Han River Pavilion* was designed as a venue for public events, such as screenings, concerts and talks, while *Euclid* and *Tribute* act as spaces of contemplation.

I'm also interested in imaginary landscapes or places of escape, such as those that are created within *Harrison's Garden* and *Just Sometimes*. For *Just Sometimes* I was asked to create an artwork on a river in Rotterdam to last for one weekend. During the complex development of *Aeolus*, it was a relief to make a quick, visually engaging artwork in response to this brief.

Treasured City

2017

Treasured City is a creative treasure hunt; a playful fusion of history, craftsmanship, mathematics, code breaking, poetry and painting.

First, Luke selected five small artefacts, which he and the curator felt represented the region, from North Lincolnshire Museum's collection. The objects, which reflected Scunthorpe's agricultural, industrial, geological and social history, spanned ancient through to modern times. Gold replicas of the objects (each worth at least £2,500) were created and then hidden across the town for the public to find and keep.

Working with a code breaker from GCHQ intelligence agency, clues to the whereabouts of the five gold objects were woven into the visual content of five paintings, which were exhibited at 20–21 Visual Arts Centre, Scunthorpe. The codes in the paintings ranged in difficulty. One was so easy to solve that even a child could work out the location of the golden treasure, while other codes were far harder to crack. Thousands of people, including code breakers from across the UK, flocked to the gallery to attempt to decipher the paintings, at times leading to a mad dash across the town (sometimes in the dead of night) to try and be the first to discover the hidden artefacts.

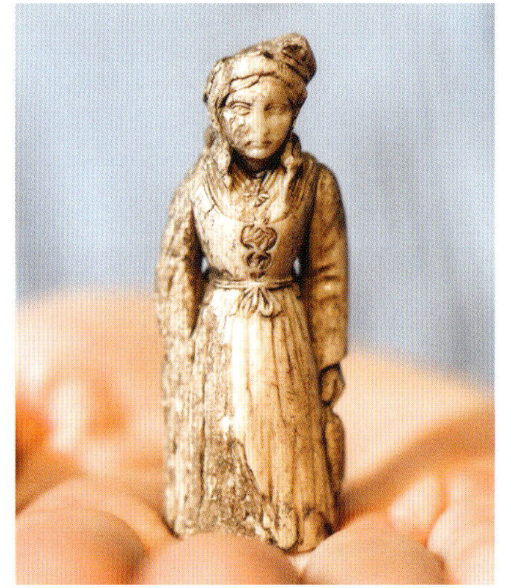

Sixteenth-century Ivory Fisherwoman from North Lincolnshire Museum

Many local people visiting the exhibition had never been to the arts centre before, and for weeks it became the 'talk of the town'. The project gained extensive news coverage both locally and nationally, which promoted Scunthorpe in a positive light as a town where exciting and creative things can happen.

Treasured City was commissioned by 20–21 Visual Arts Centre, Scunthorpe, with funding from Arts Council England.

LJ: *I like the idea that ancient objects that were once hidden beneath the earth and then later discovered and displayed at the museum, were re-hidden.*

▶ *Five 18-carat gold cast objects*

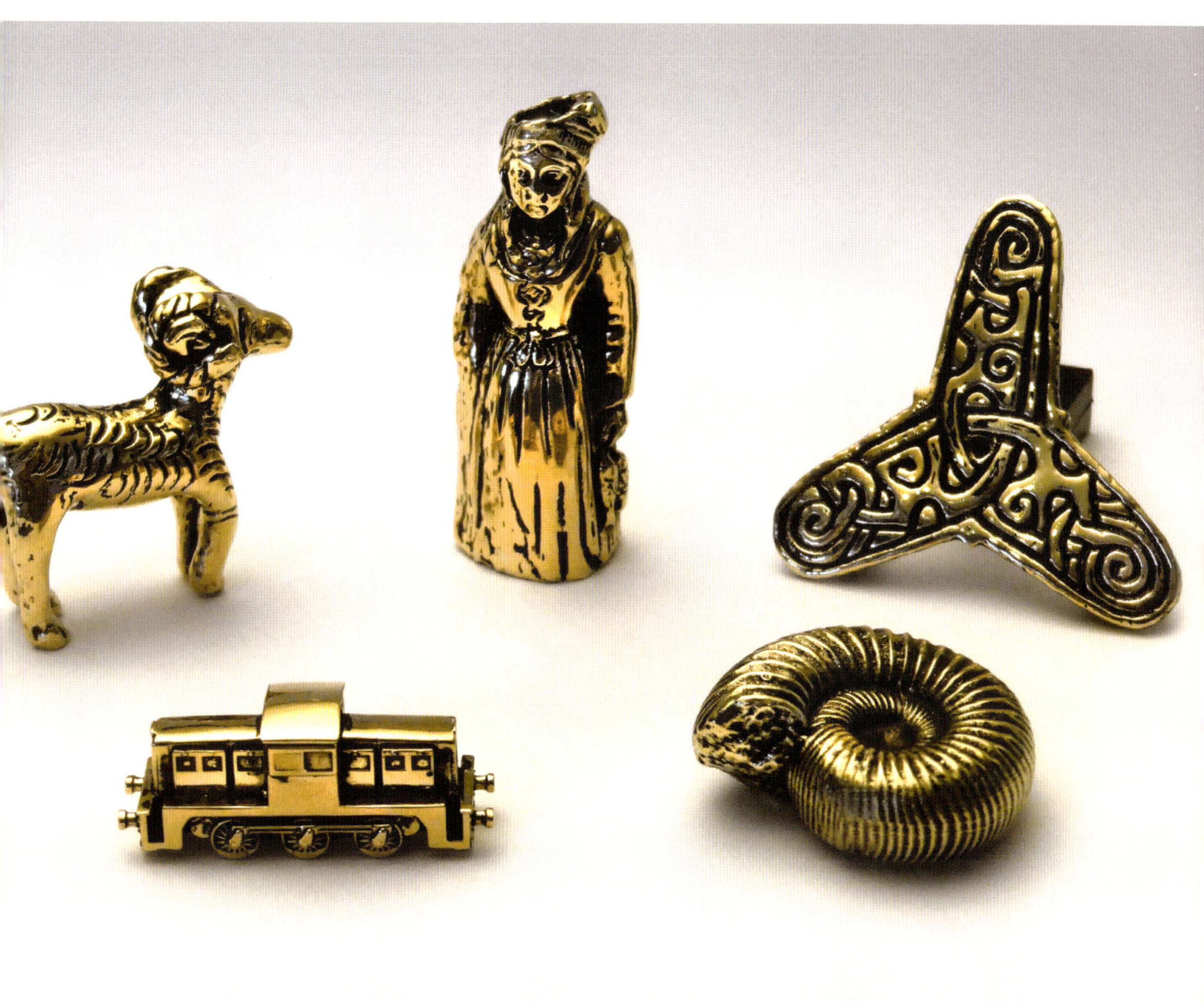

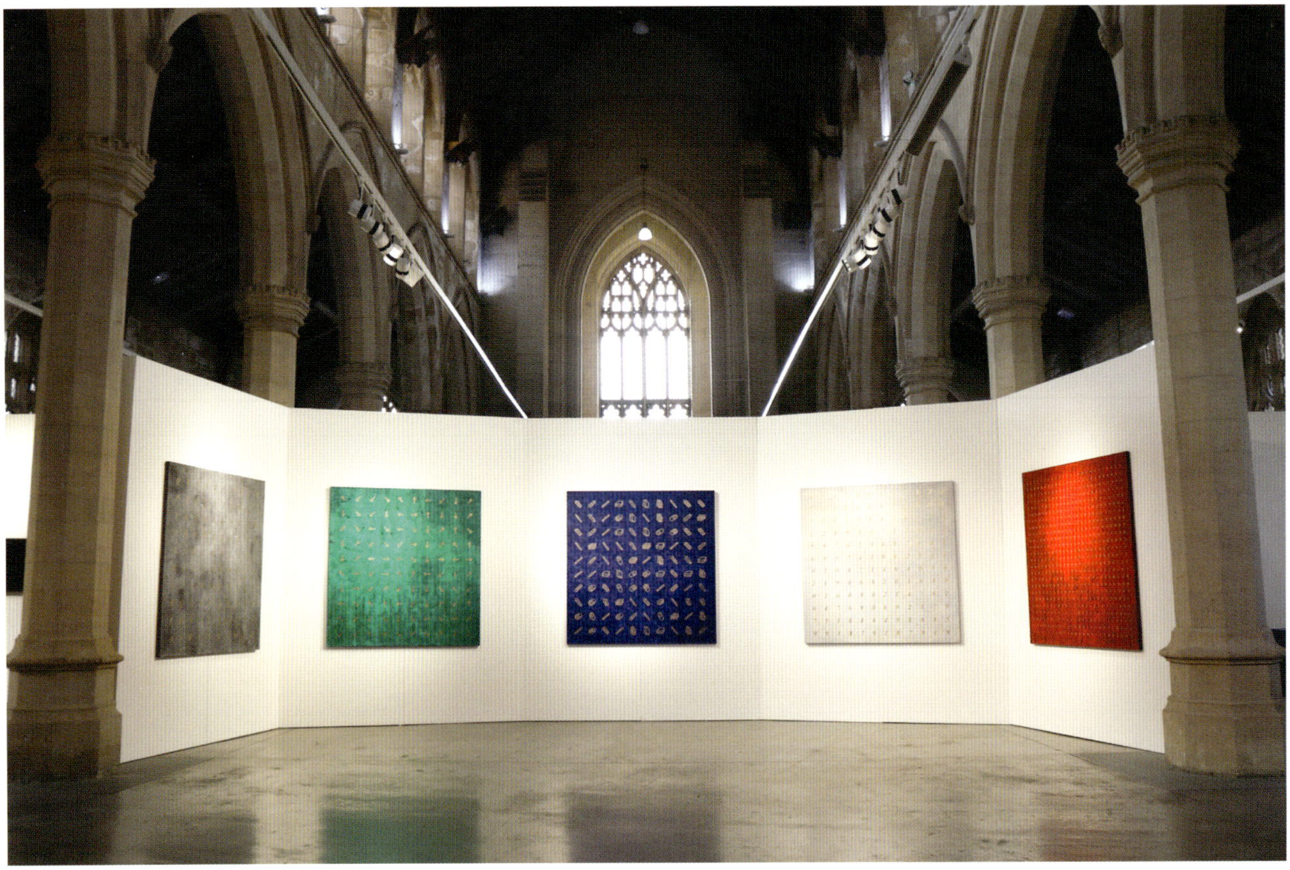

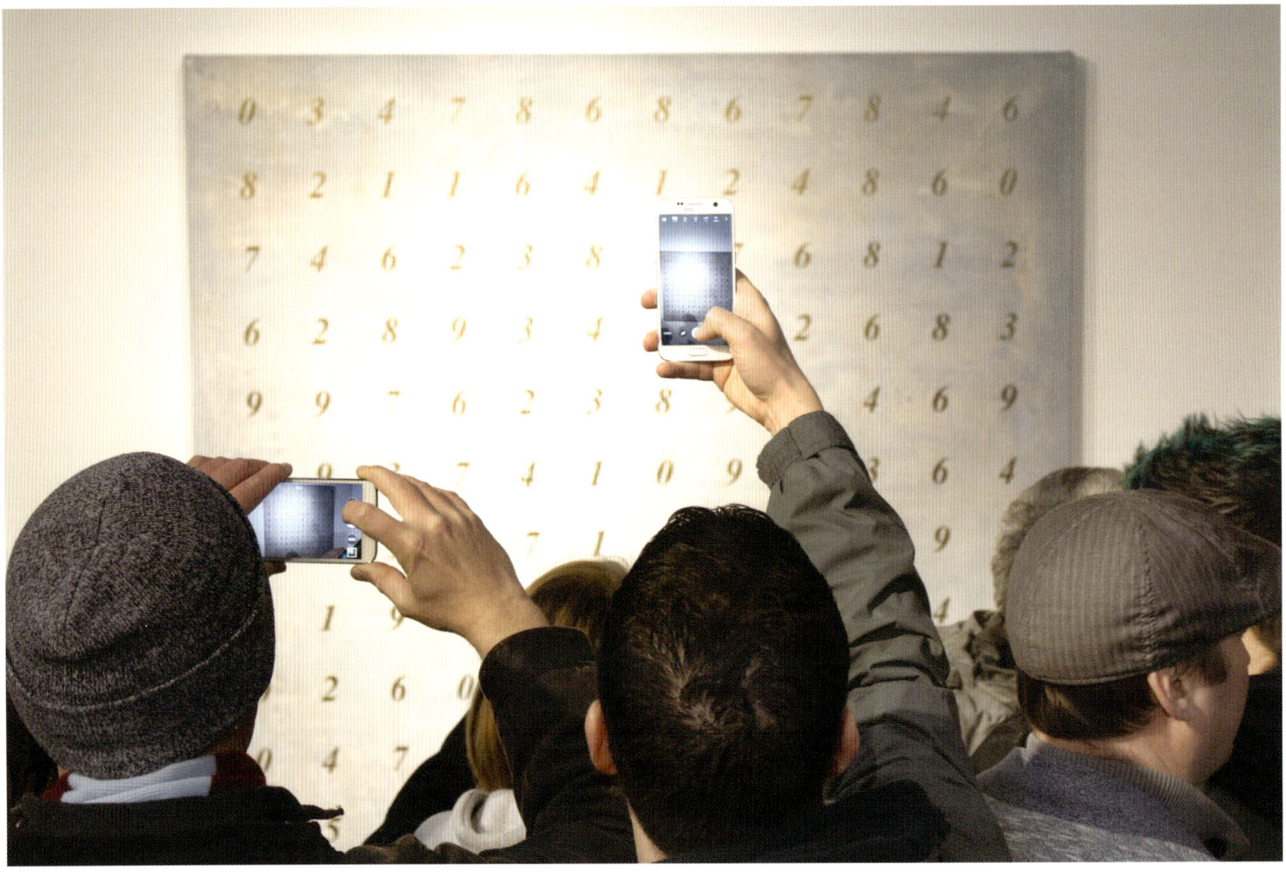

Paintings exhibited at 20–21 Visual Arts Centre, Scunthorpe, 2017

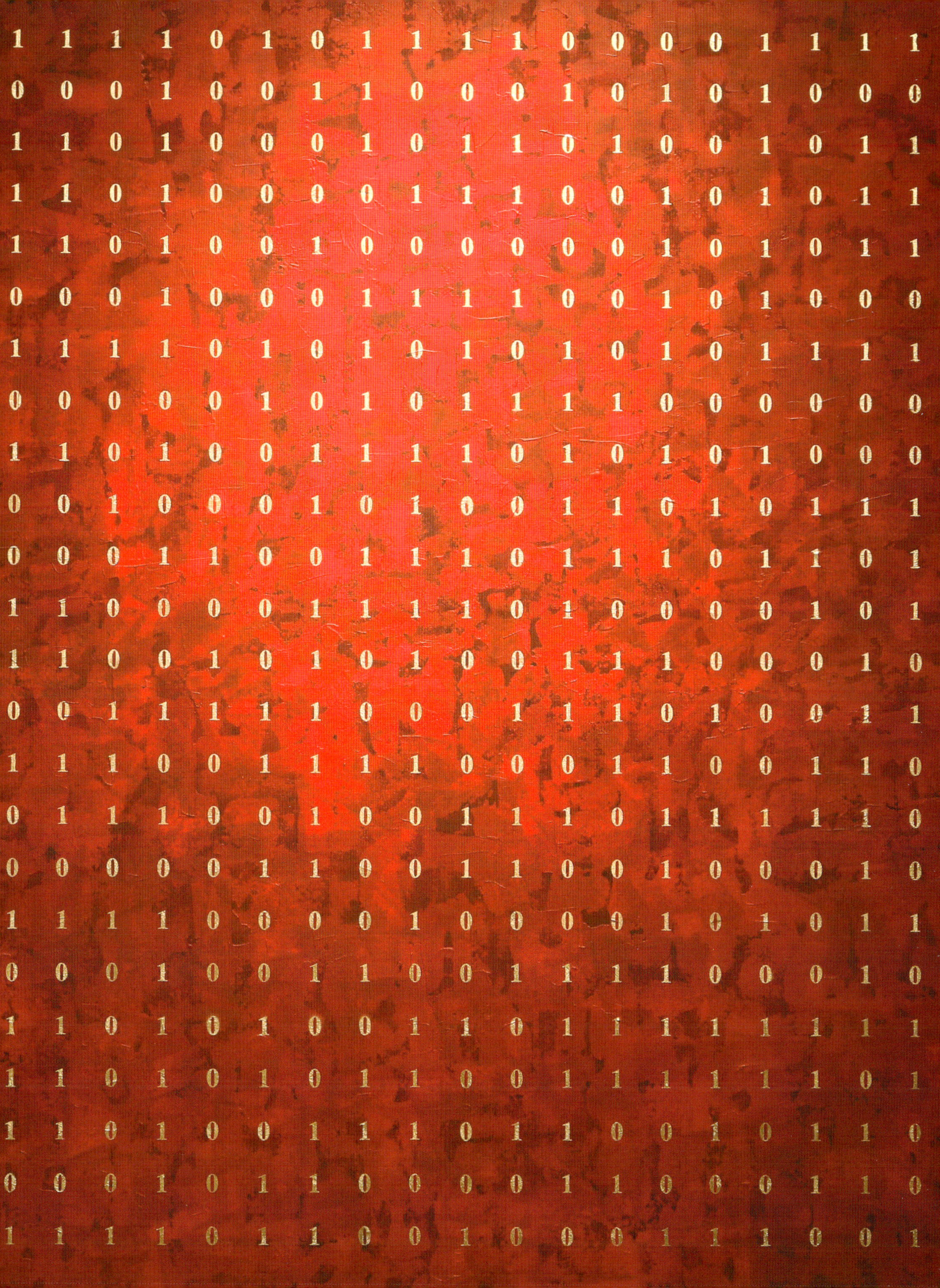

Harrison's Garden

2015–2019

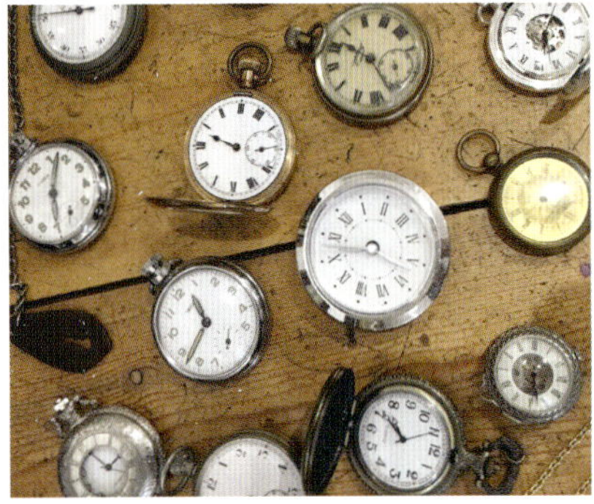

The Ropewalk, Barton-upon-Humber, 2019

Harrison's Garden is an installation of clocks and an imagined landscape. The title of the installation refers to the famous clockmaker John Harrison (1693–1776), who struggled for decades to make navigation at sea safer and ended up creating the most accurate clock the world had ever seen.

The work incorporates around 3,000 clocks and other timepieces, which have been clustered into 'species' to form islands, pathways and borders. Many of the clocks in the installation were donated by the public, each carrying their own personal story and significance. Some clocks seem like classics of their time, others are a pastiche pretending to be classical clocks from a previous era. Some are on the march, while others seem to be in conversation with one another. Clicking and ticking, they create a rhythmic, and at times unnerving, landscape of sound.

▶ *Penrhyn Castle, Wales, 2018*

Modern society has developed, and arguably only been made possible, through the timepieces that surround us. We wake up, work, eat and sleep according to time. Each with our own body clock, we calibrate ourselves every day through the man-made clocks that surround us. Many of these analogue clocks have now lost their value and function, in part replaced by mobile phones, computers and other digital technology.

Harrison's Garden was commissioned by Connect! and first presented at Thelma Hulbert Gallery, Devon. With clocks being added by the public at each consecutive presentation, it then toured to four National Trust properties across the UK, including Nostell Priory where it was exhibited alongside one of John Harrison's original working wooden clocks. Its final presentation was at The Ropewalk, Barton-upon-Humber, after which the clocks were auctioned off to raise money for a statue of John Harrison for the town.

LJ: *The installation can perhaps be seen as a reminder that we are all here, simultaneously moving through time together.*

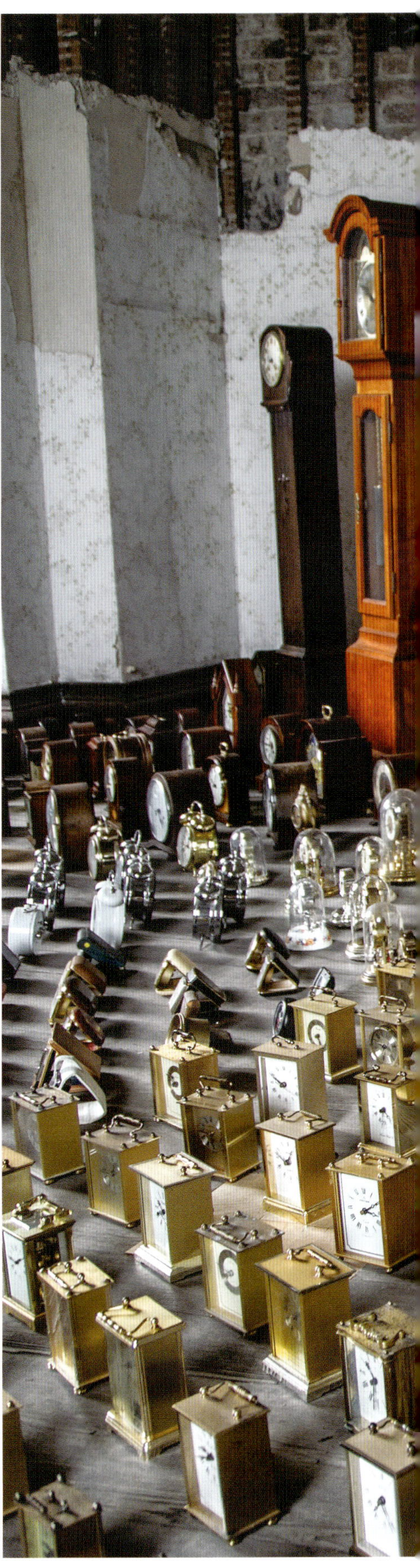

"

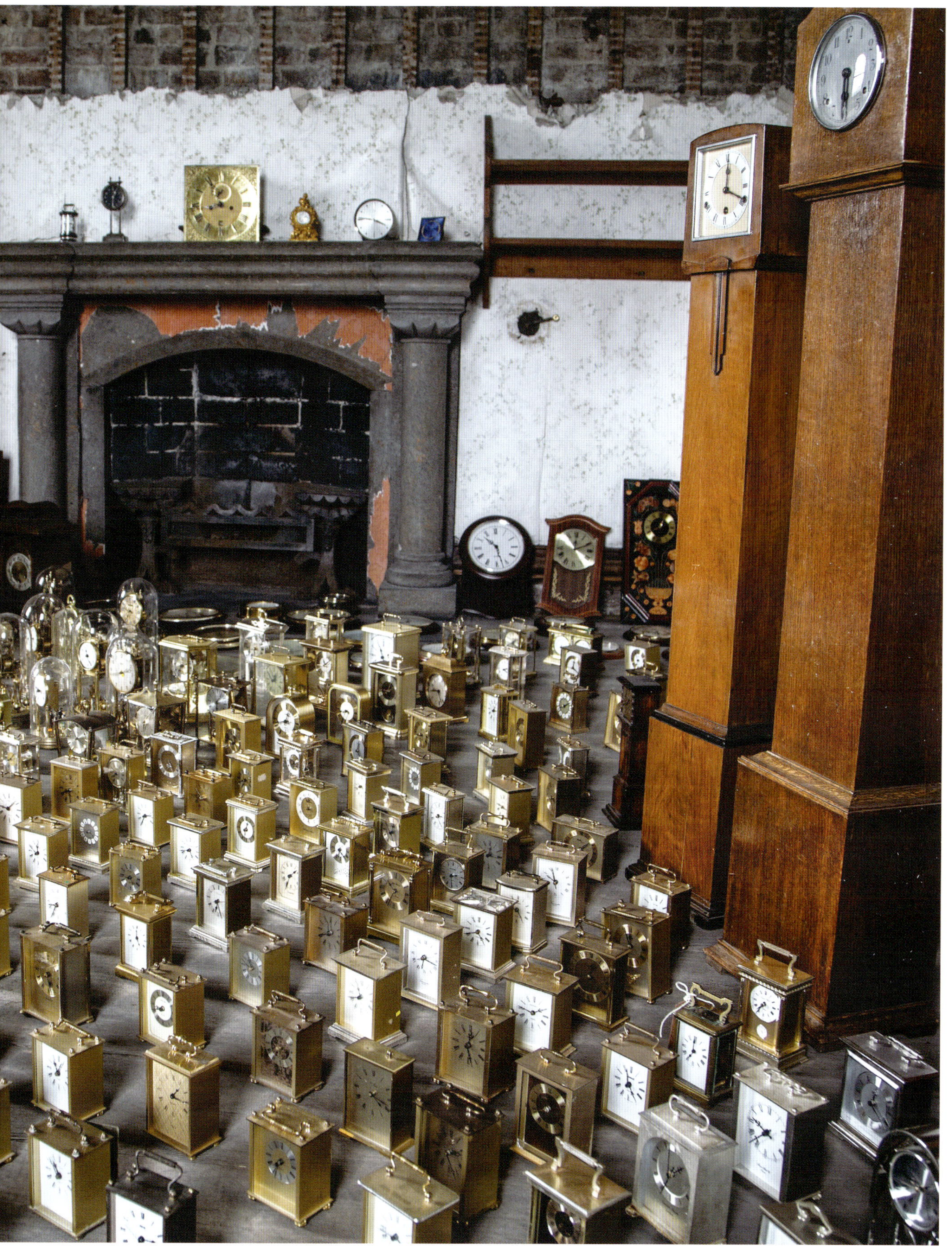

Just Sometimes
2010

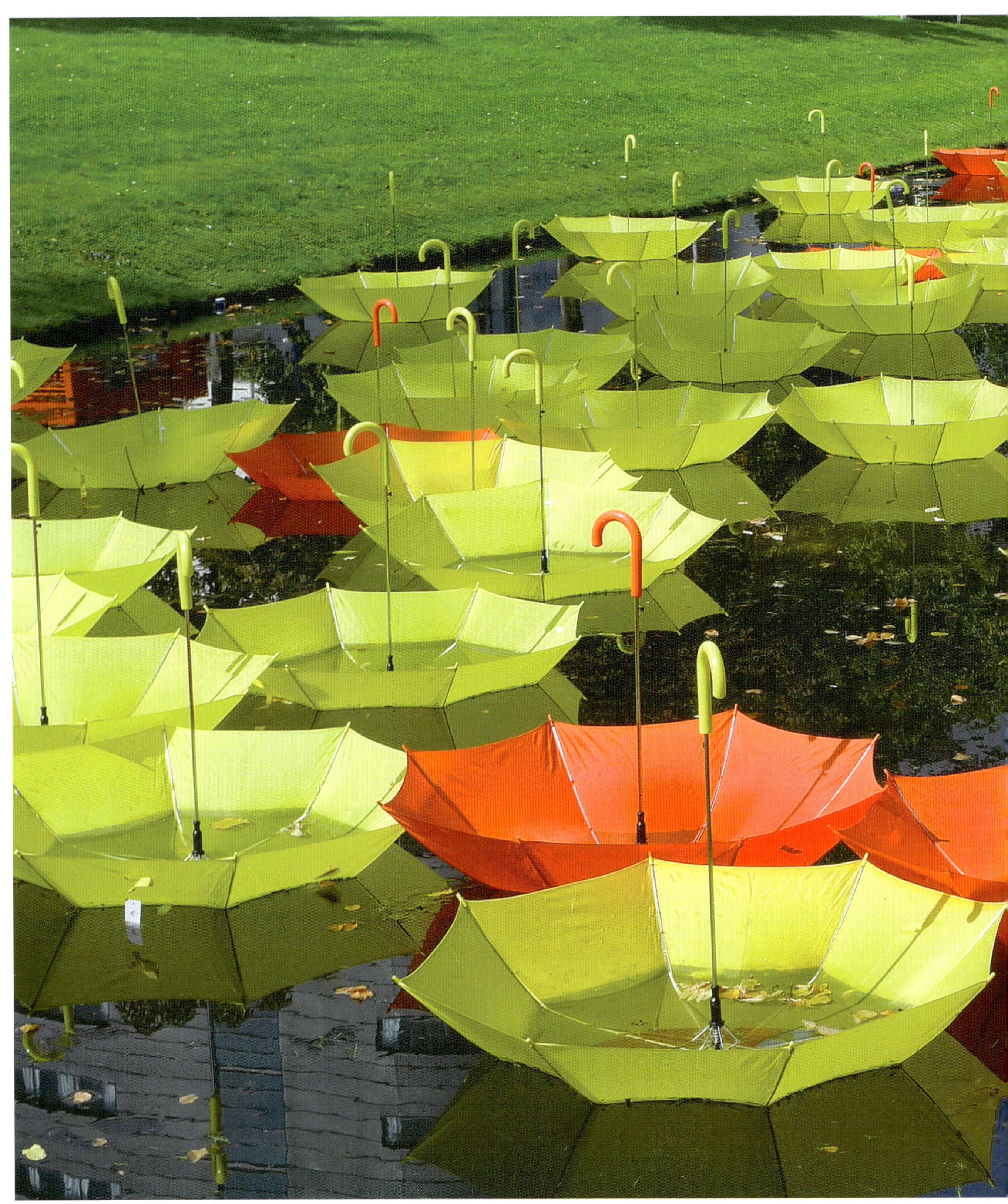

Witte de With Festival, Rotterdam

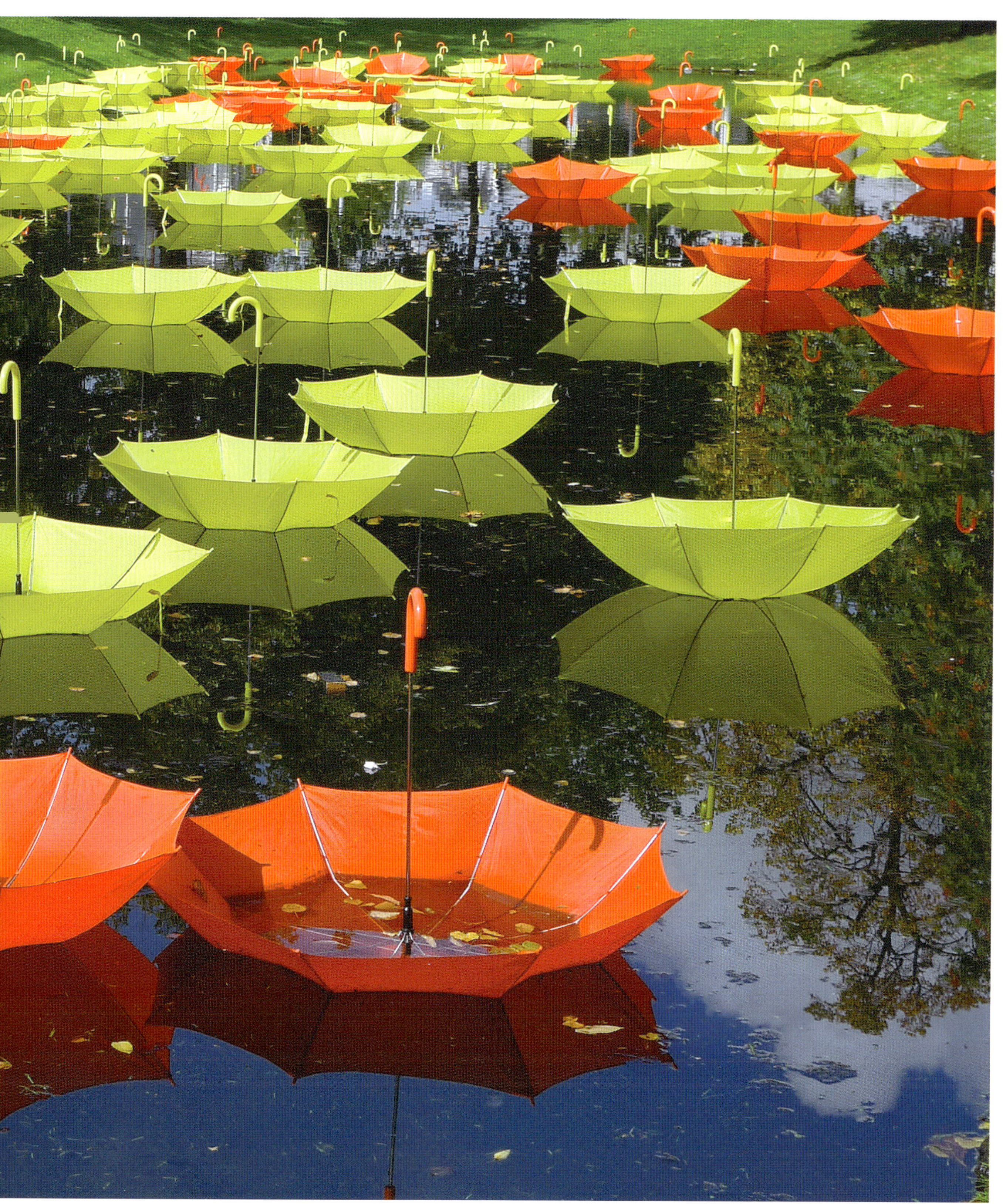

Euclid

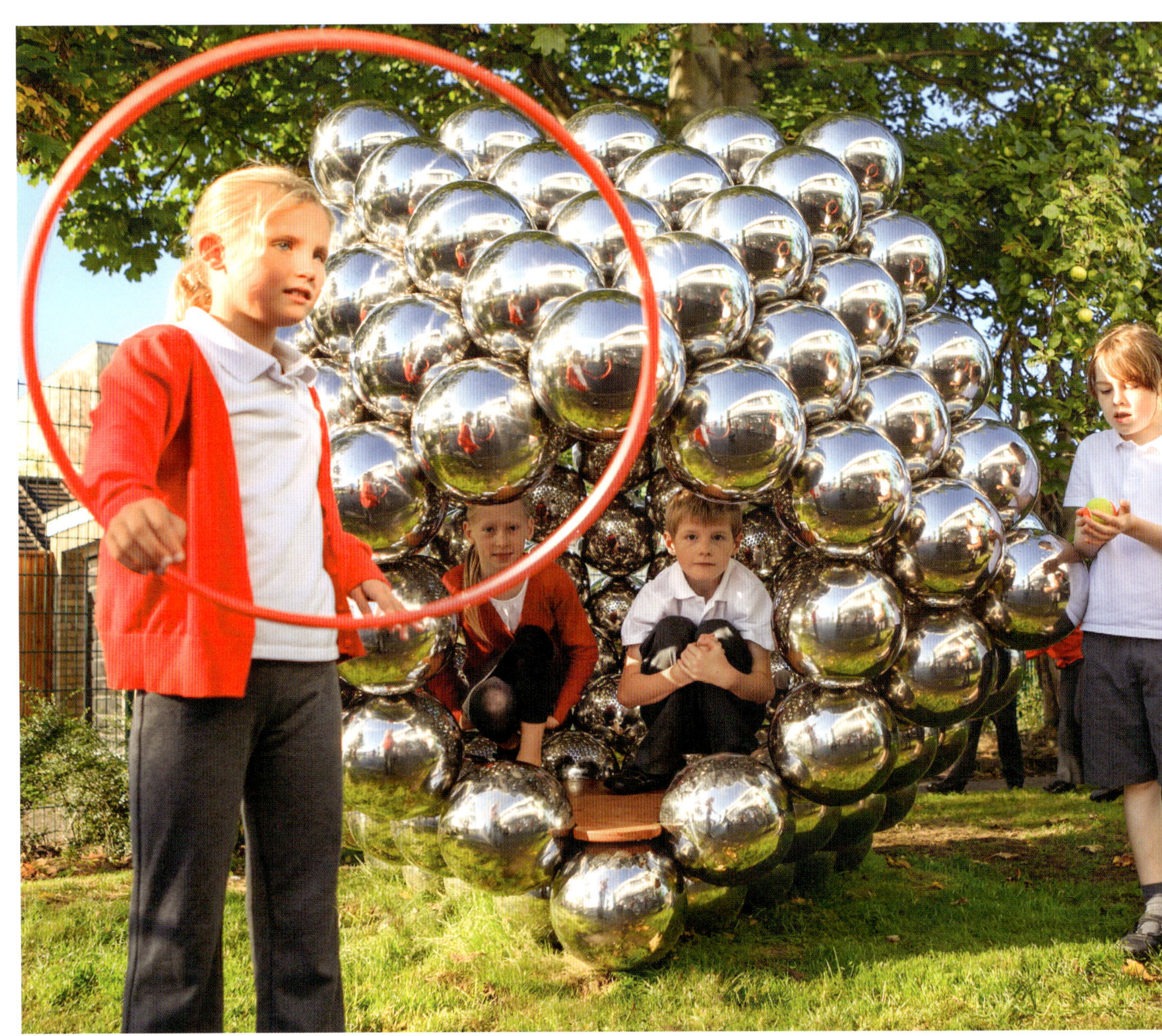

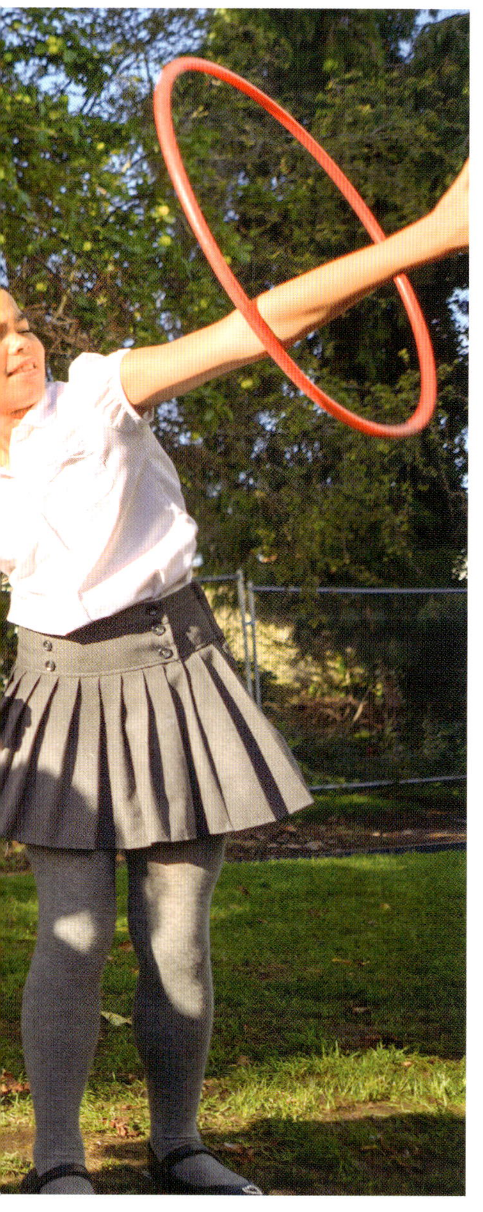

Euclid is a large, mirrored, stainless steel structure, which was commissioned for a new primary school in Bristol. The design grew out of a series of workshops, which Luke ran with children who were going to be using the new school. Together, they designed and built 1:50 scaled architectural structures and thought about how they might be used. The children wanted a den, a private space and somewhere fun to hide. During one of these workshops, Luke saw a child playing with some magnetic balls, which influenced the final design of the artwork.

Euclid was a Greek mathematician, often referred to as the 'Father of Geometry'. His work, *The Elements,* is one of the most influential in the history of mathematics, serving as the main textbook for teaching mathematics (especially geometry) from the time of its publication in 300BC until the late nineteenth or early twentieth-century. The *Euclid* sculpture is an icosahedron, one of the five platonic solids, described in Euclid's *Book XIII, Proposition 16.*

Euclid was commissioned by Arnolfini, as part of Bristol City Council's Primary Capital Programme.

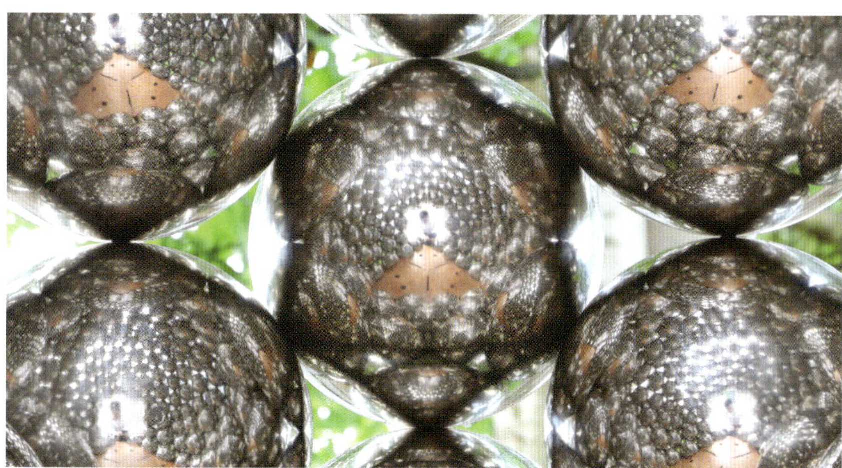

LJ: *Whilst expressing my interest in the microscopic world, the artwork is a fusion of geometry, optics and engineering. Acting as a contemplation space for children to climb inside, the structure reflects itself, the children, and the surrounding landscape of the school.*

Tribute

2017

Tribute was created for the main reception area of the new Royal Liverpool University Hospital to celebrate, remember, and give thanks to the generosity of organ and tissue donors and their families.

Through its round, tower-like form, the artwork acts as an internal landmark and focal point within the building. Beautiful patterns of coloured light emanating from the semi-transparent structure can be viewed and enjoyed from all angles, altering with the changing daylight streaming into the atrium from above.

A doorway in its side invites visitors to enter and stand, or sit on the in-built seating. Many of the translucent coloured panels have printed text on them. These include extracts from personal responses and stories collected from patients and staff of the hospital, illustrating the impact which organ and tissue donation has had on their lives. A mirrored ceiling and reflective floor make the space within the structure appear infinite, creating an inspiring space for contemplation.

The artwork is designed to be experienced and appreciated by everyone visiting the hospital. Some may simply enjoy the geometry, colours and reflections, while others will stop to read the stories, which remember and give thanks to the generosity of organ and tissue donors and their families.

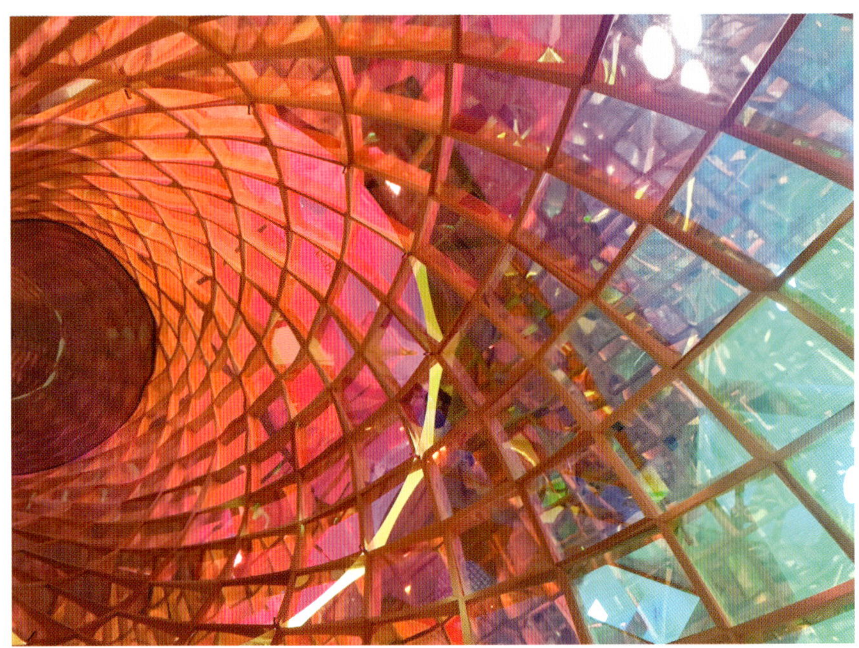

Detail

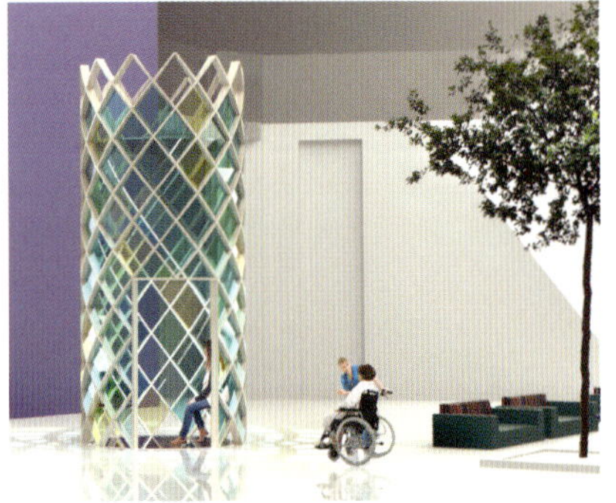

CAD mock-up

Tribute was commissioned by the Royal Liverpool and Broadgreen University Hospitals' Organ Donation Committee and Royal Liverpool Dialysis Utilities Fund. It was fabricated with the craftsmanship of John Hall, Richard Stump, 4th Dimension, Vicki Leach and Kings Plastics. Unfortunately the construction company Carillion (who were managing the build of the new hospital) went bust just after the artwork was installed so it is yet to be unveiled to the public.

▶ *Under construction*

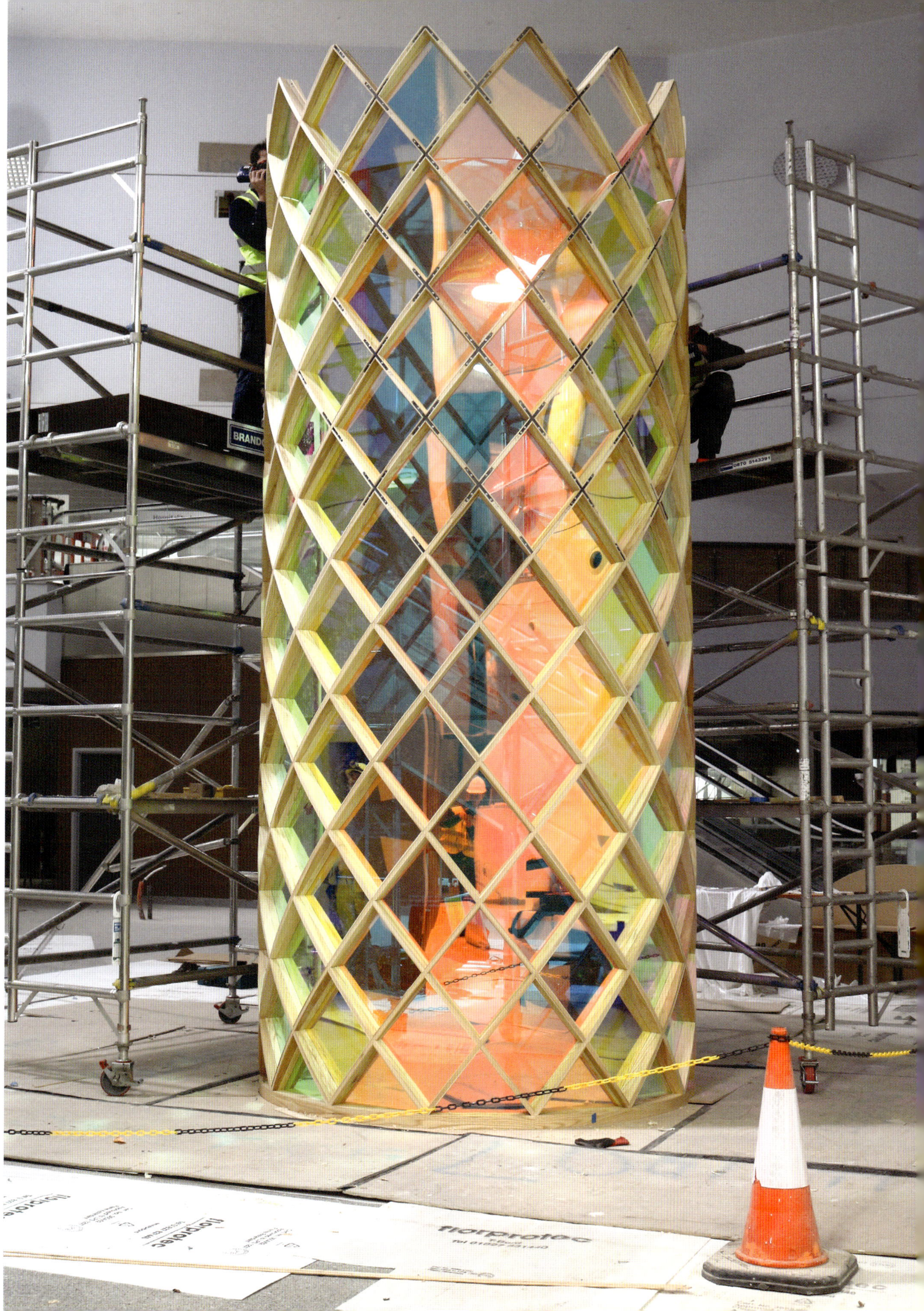

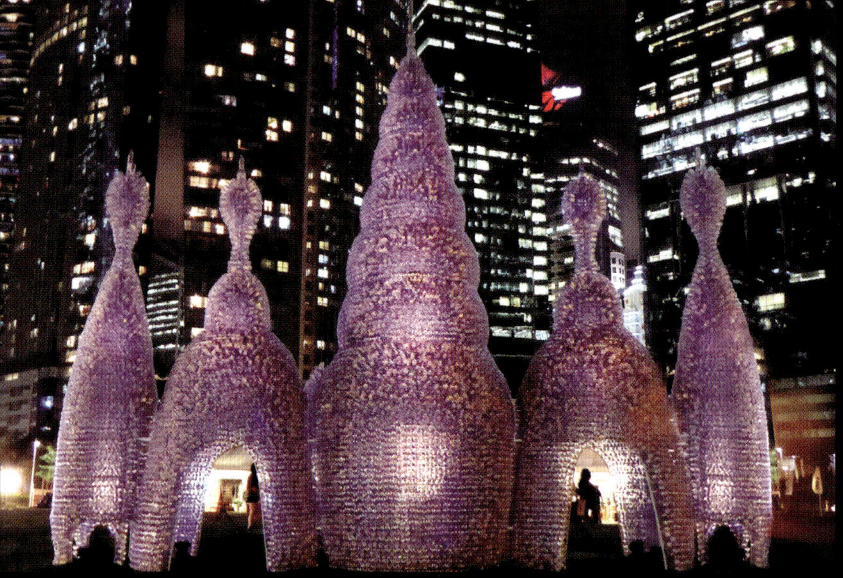

Ocean Pavilion was a temporary
structure created for *i Light Festival*
in Singapore. Made from 25,000 used
plastic water bottles collected in
Singapore, the form of the pavilion was
inspired by microscopic underwater
creatures called radiolarians which
are found in the nearby Singapore
Strait. During the night it was internally
illuminated, creating the effect of a
glowing temple and marine lifeform
for the public to explore.

Made with the help of 11 schools
and a local institute for ex-offenders,
the artwork promotes the reuse and
recycling of materials, but also considers
the devastating effect plastic has on our
ocean environment. At the end of this
project all the bottles were recycled.

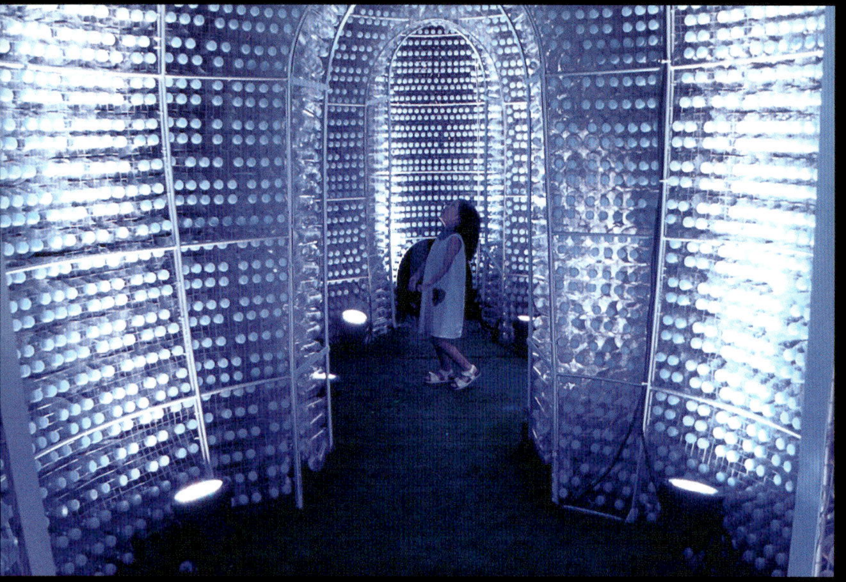

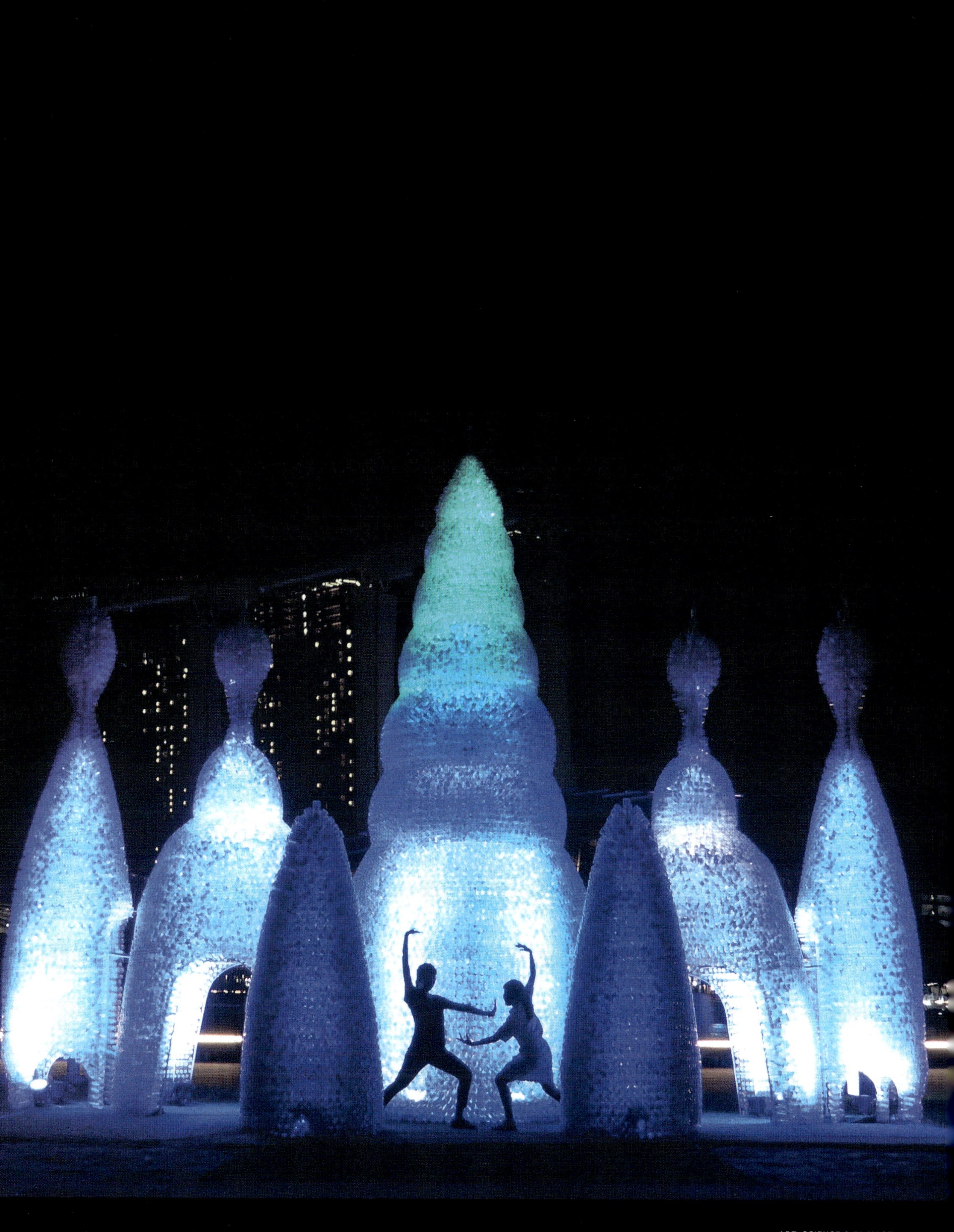

Han River Pavilion
2018

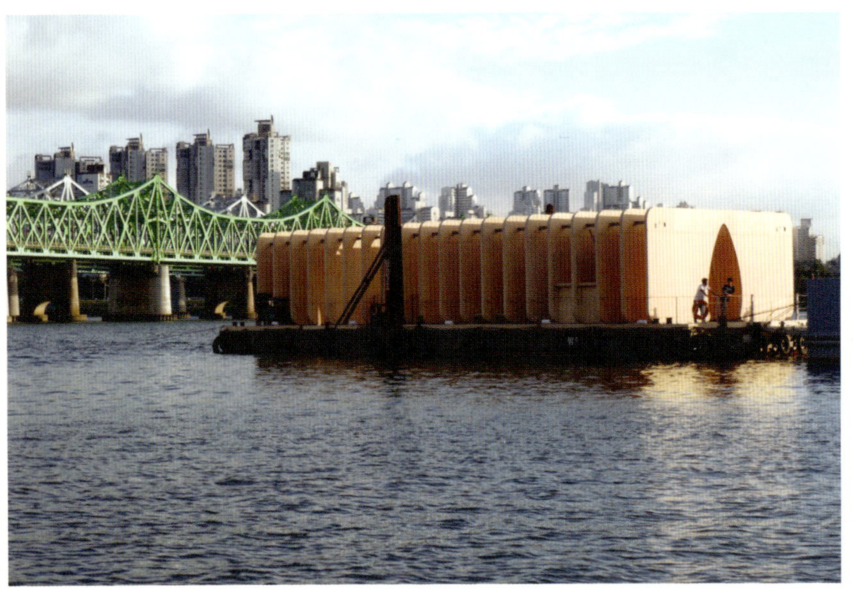

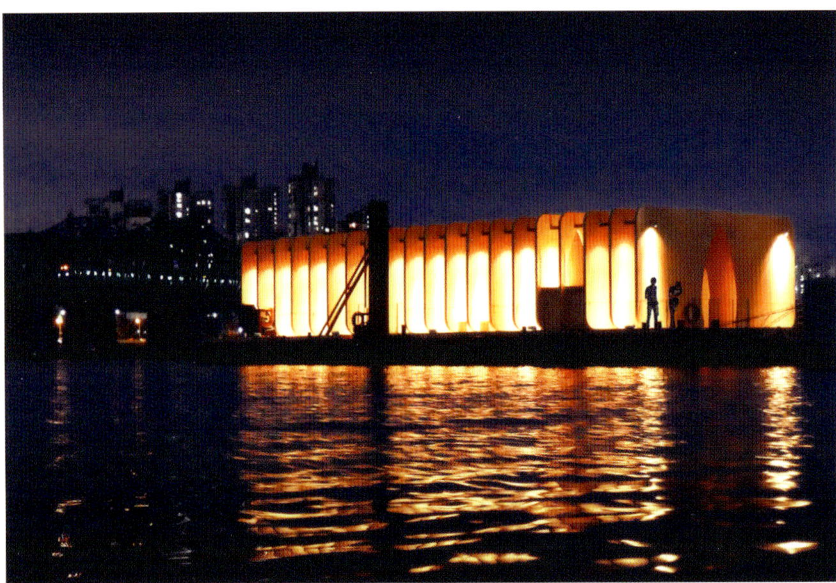

Created for Hangang Art Park in Seoul, South Korea, the *Han River Pavilion* was designed as an events space as well as a location for exploration and contemplation. Like many of Luke's artworks, *Han River Pavilion* is completed by the presence of the public. As a venue for concerts, film screenings and lectures, the pavilion became a space for participation and activation; a destination where the local community could connect, express themselves, and grow together. Accessed from a walkway connected to the riverbank, the public were able to explore the structure both day and night.

The *Pavilion's* form was inspired by looking at the microscopic diatoms (algae) found in the Han River. Affected by pollution, diatoms are used by scientists as bioindicators to study the health of water systems. To design the pavilion, enlarged versions of these geometric natural forms were carved out from an oblong built on top of the barge.

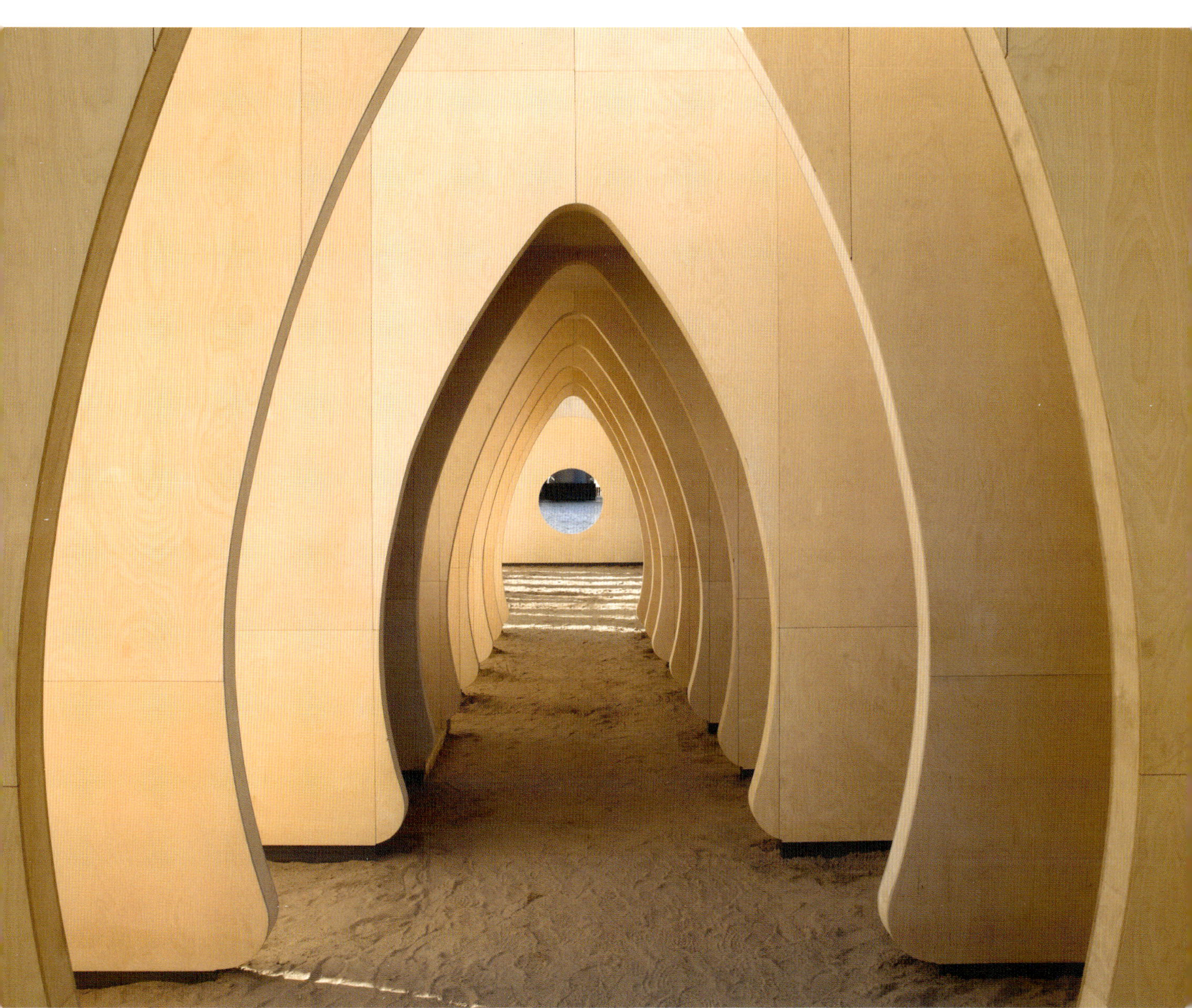

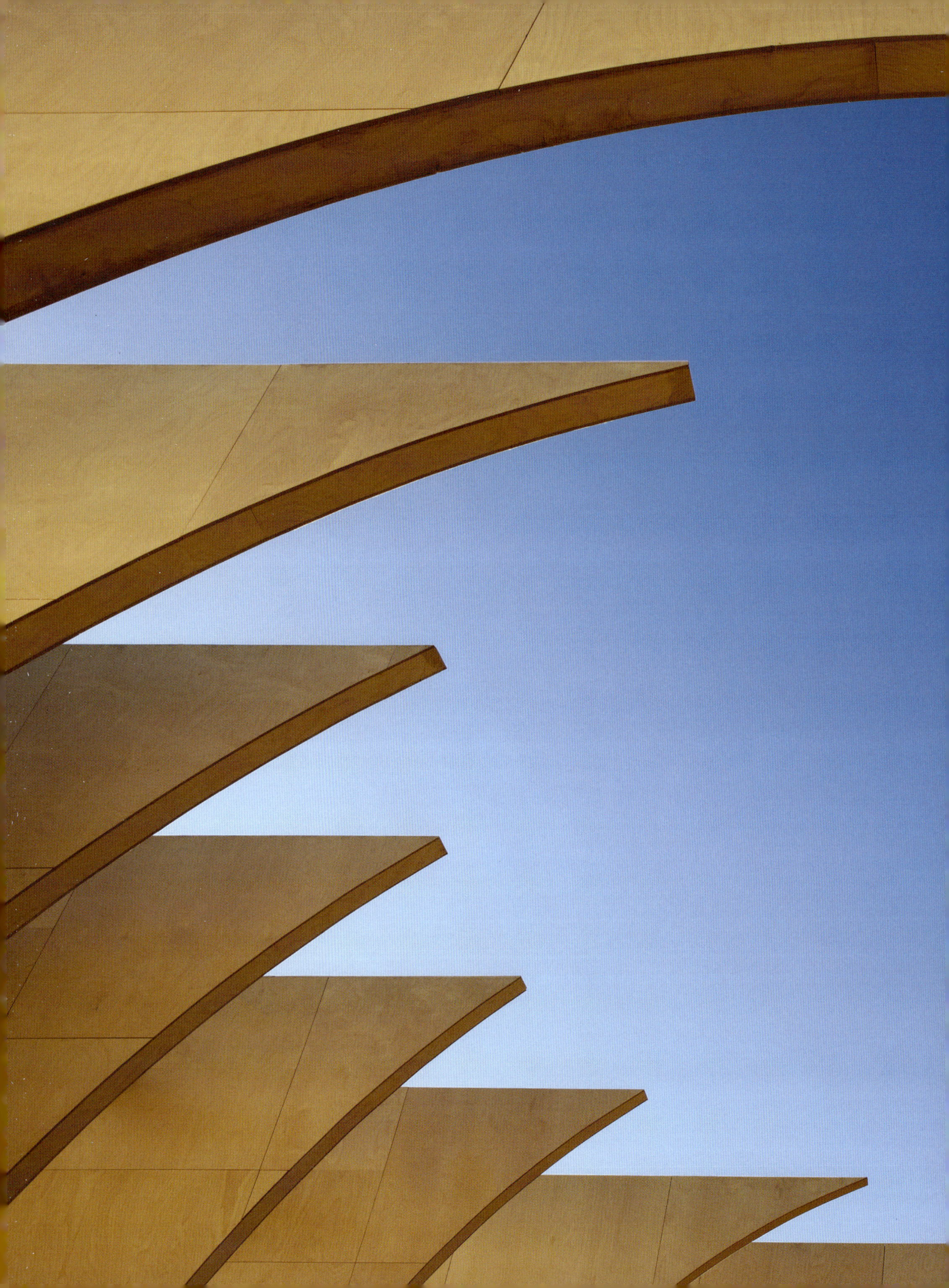

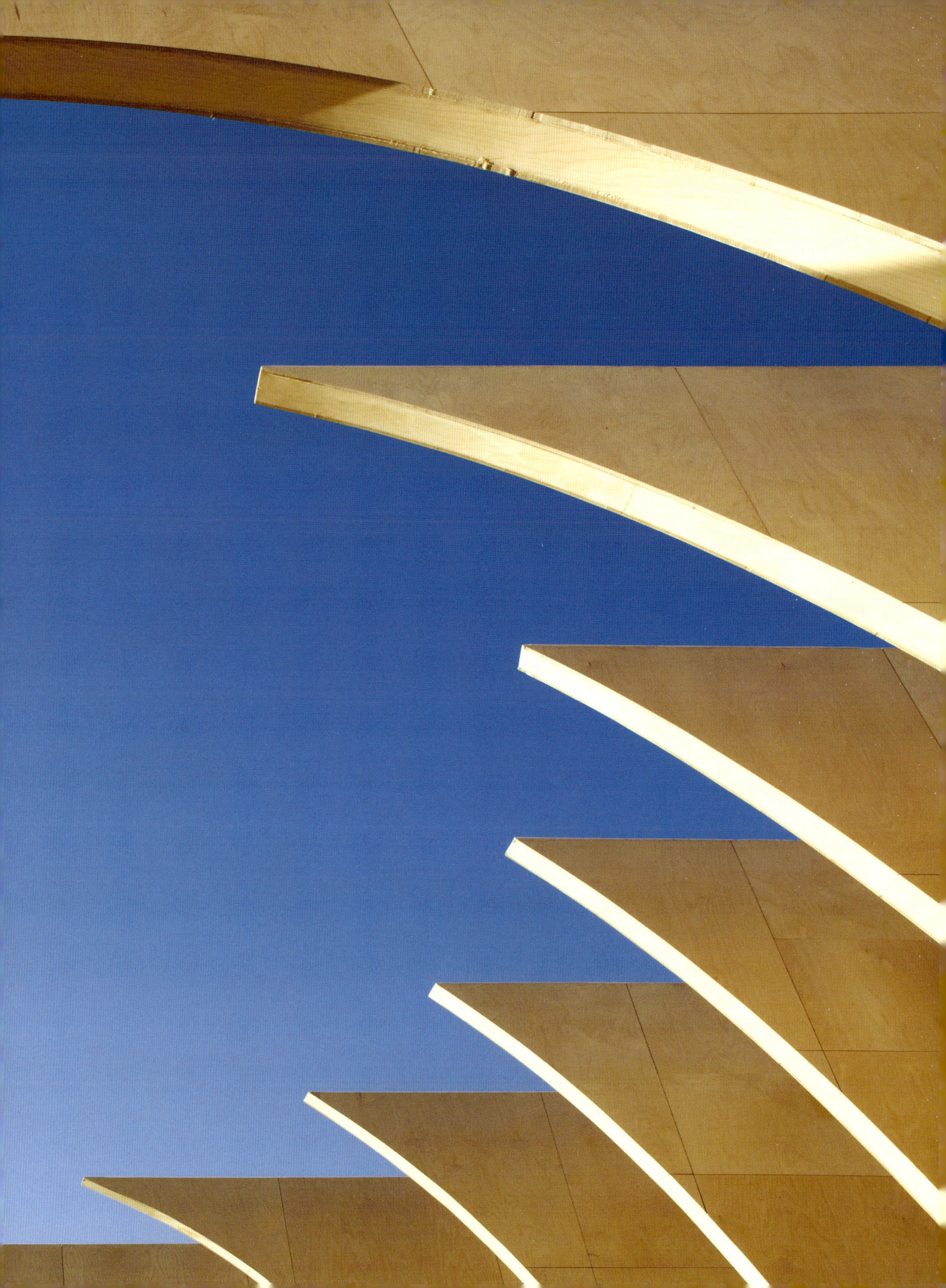

Artworks

Retinal Memory Volume, 1997, installation, commissioned by *European Media Art Festival* with support from University of Wales Optometry Department

Matrix, 2001, installation, co-commissioned by Site Gallery and VIVID, UK

Tide, 2001, installation, commissioned by DA2 Digital Arts Development Agency with support from the Institute of Physics and Arts Council England

Sky Orchestra, 2003–2013, live artwork, originally funded by Nesta, UK

Dream Concert, 2004–2007, live artwork, originally commissioned by *Fierce Festival*, UK, with support from Think Tank, Nesta and DA2 Digital Arts Development Agency

Ghost Plane, 2004, installation, commissioned by Arts Catalyst, UK

Glass Microbiology, ongoing since 2004, glass sculptures, originally funded by Nesta. Museum collections include Metropolitan Museum of Art, New York, USA; European Museum of Modern Glass, Germany; Natural History Museum, Kuwait; Museum of Glass, Washington, USA; Knoxville Museum of Art, USA; Shanghai Museum of Glass, China; Wellcome Collection, London, UK; Museum of Health and Medicine, University of Tokyo, Japan

Wellcome Portrait, 2004, limited edition print, commissioned by Wellcome Trust, UK

Tunnel Vision, 2006, installation, commissioned for *Brunel 200*, with support from the Millennium Commission, Heritage Lottery Fund, Arts Council England, Arts and Business, Business West, South Gloucestershire Council, Motaman and JVC

Dream Director, 2007, live artwork, commissioned by Watershed with support from Arts Council England

St. Gabriel's Garden, 2007, installation, commissioned by *Fierce Festival*, UK

Talking Ring, 2007, sculpture

Falling Man, 2008, live artwork

Play Me, I'm Yours, 2008–2019, installation, originally commissioned by *Fierce Festival*, UK

Portrait Projecting Ring, 2008, sculpture

Plant Orchestra, 2009–2011, installation, originally commissioned by Night Jar, UK

Just Sometimes, 2010, installation, commissioned by *Witte de With Festival*, Rotterdam, Netherlands

My RSC Gallery, 2010, installation, commissioned by Royal Shakespeare Company, UK

Piano Nocturne, 2010, live artwork, commissioned by *City of London Festival* and Polish Cultural Institute, London, UK for *Chopin200*

Aeolus, 2011–2012, originally commissioned by Institute of Sound and Vibration Research at the University of Southampton and the Acoustics Research Centre at the University of Salford, UK, with support from Engineering and Physical Sciences Research Council, Arts Council England and Outokumpu, Finland

Tōhoku Japanese Earthquake, 2011, sculpture, commissioned by Jerwood Visual Arts and Grizedale Arts, UK

Kinetic Chandeliers, 2012–2014, glass sculptures, originally commissioned

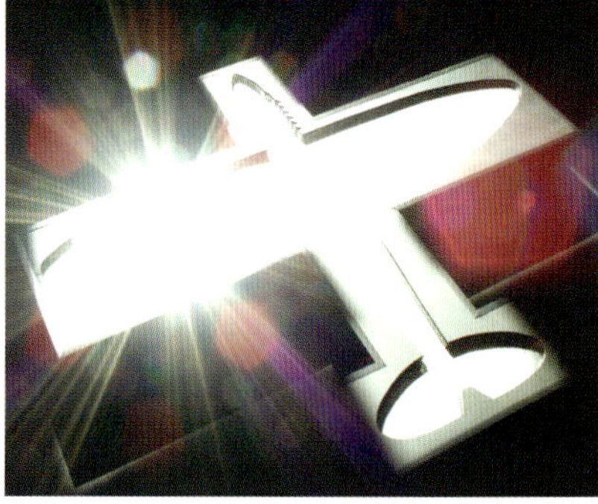

Ghost Plane | *2004*

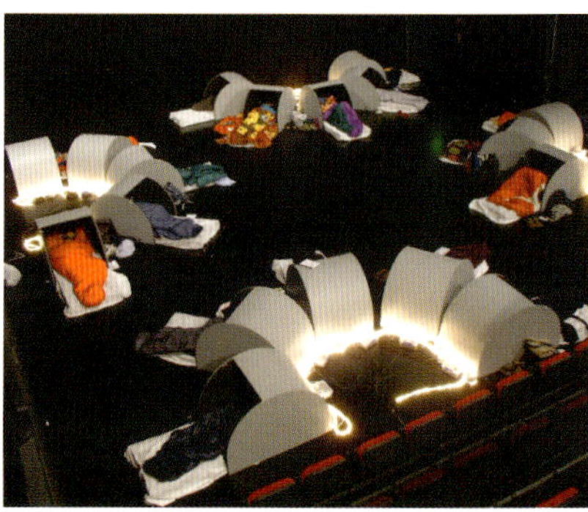

Dream Director | *2007*

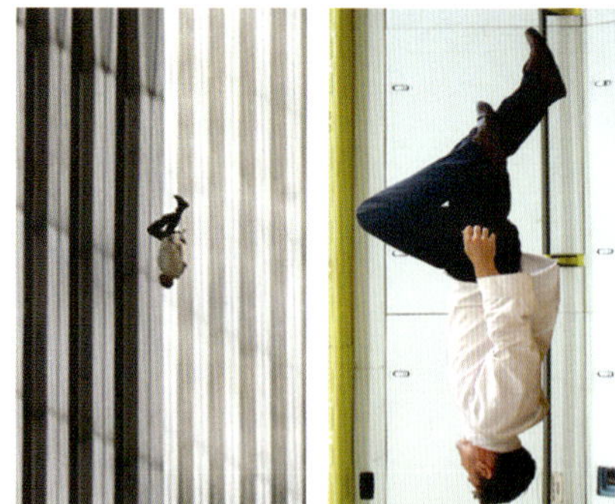

Falling Man | *2008*

for Bristol and Bath Science Park, UK, included in collection of Chrysler Museum, USA

Stock Exchange Data, 2012, glass sculptures, included in collection of Museum of Glass, Washington, USA

Lullaby, 2013–2015, live artwork, originally commissioned by Sustrans, UK

Maya, 2013, sculpture, a Bristol Temple Quarter commission coordinated by Watershed, Knowle West Media Centre and MAYK, UK, with support from Bristol City Council and Arts Council England

Park and Slide, 2014, installation, commissioned by Bristol City Council for *Make Sundays Special*, with support from crowdfunding, UK

Harrison's Garden, 2015–2019, installation, originally commissioned by Connect! in partnership with Thelma Hulbert Gallery, UK and National Trust

E. coli, 2015, sculpture, commissioned by The University of Sheffield, UK for *KrebsFest*

Euclid, 2015, sculpture, a Primary Capital Commission for Southville Primary School developed by Arnolfini, in partnership with Bristol City Council and the Bristol Local Education Partnership, UK

Invisible Homeless, 2015, glass sculpture, commissioned by Glass Hub, UK with support from Arts Council England

Withdrawn, 2015, installation, commissioned by National Trust for Trust New Art Bristol in partnership with Forestry Commission England, with support from Arts Council England

Museum of the Moon, ongoing since 2016, installation, co-commissioned by a number of creative organisations brought together by Luke Jerram and *Norfolk & Norwich Festival*, including *Greenwich+Docklands International Festival, Brighton Festival*, Without Walls, *Cork Midsummer Festival*, At-Bristol, *Lakes Alive*, Provinciaal Domein Dommelhof, *Les Tombées de la Nuit*, Rennes, and Kimmel Center for the Performing Arts. Created in partnership with the UK Space Agency, University of Bristol and The Association for Science and Discovery Centres. Part of the European INSITU network. Museum collections include CosmoCaixa, Barcelona; Houston Museum of Natural Sciences, USA; Museum of Applied Arts and Sciences, Sydney and Questacon, Canberra, Australia

Ocean Pavilion, 2017, installation, commissioned by *i Light Festival*, Singapore

Treasured City, 2017, painting and sculpture, commissioned by 20–21 Visual Arts Centre, UK, with support from Arts Council England and North Lincolnshire Museum, UK

Tribute, 2017, installation, commissioned by the Royal Liverpool and Broadgreen University Hospitals' Organ Donation Committee and Royal Liverpool Dialysis Utilities Fund, Ireland

1000 Flowers, 2018, live artwork, commissioned by *Cork Midsummer Festival*, Ireland

Apollo, 2018, sculpture, commissioned by St Georges, Bristol, UK

Gaia, since 2018, installation, co-commissioned by Natural Environment Research Council (NERC), *Bluedot Festival* and the UK Association for Science and Discovery Centres

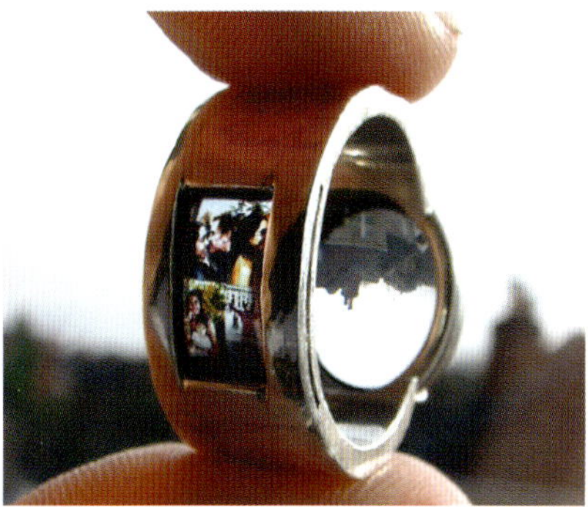

Portrait Projecting Ring | *2008*

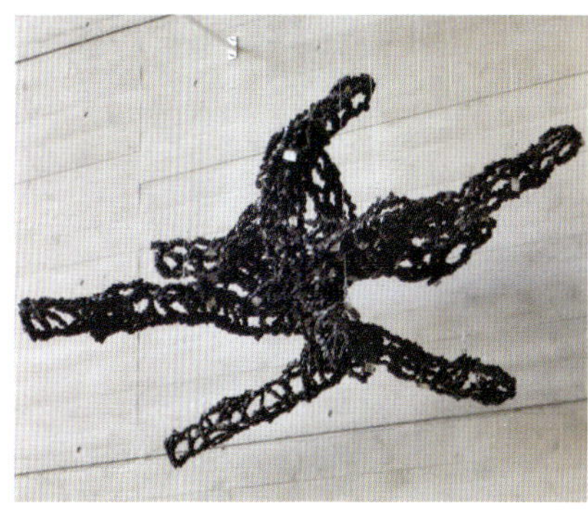

Inhale | *2018*

Han River Pavilion, 2018, installation, commissioned by Hangang Art Park, Seoul, South Korea

Impossible Garden, 2018, installation, commissioned by Bristol Vision Institute for University of Bristol Botanic Garden, UK, with support from Leverhulme Trust

Inhale, 2018, sculpture, commissioned by University of the West of England for Our City Our Health, with support from Wellcome Trust and included in collection of We the Curious, UK

Image credits

Front cover: *Museum of the Moon*, 2018. *Culture Liverpool* at Liverpool Cathedral. Photo © Gareth Jones

Title page: *Play Me, I'm Yours*, 2014. Paris, France. Photo © Gael

p.6. *Park and Slide*, 2014. Photo © Luke Jerram

p.8. *Swine Flu*, 2009. Photo © Wellcome Collection

p.10. *Invisible Homeless*, 2015. Photo © Marc Simmons

p.12. *Talking Ring*, 2007. Photo © Luke Jerram

p.13. *1000 Flowers*, 2018. *Cork Midsummer Festival*, Ireland. Photo © Clare Keogh

p.13. *Retinal Memory Volume*, 1997. Photo © Luke Jerram

p.13. *Wellcome Portrait*, 2004. Photo © Luke Jerram

p.14. *Museum of the Moon*, 2017. University of Bristol, UK. Photo © Luke Jerram

pp.16, 17 and 18 (top and bottom). *Sky Orchestra*, 2005. Yverdon, Switzerland. Photos © Thierry Groben

p.18 (middle). *Sky Orchestra*, 2005. Yverdon, Switzerland. Photo © Fabrice Coffrini

p.19. *Sky Orchestra*, 2011. London, for the 2012 Olympic Games. Photo © Luke Jerram

p.20. *Play Me, I'm Yours*, 2008. São Paulo, Brazil. Photo © Caio Buni

p.21. *Play Me, I'm Yours*, 2009. Bristol, UK. Photo © Luke Jerram

pp.22–3. *Play Me, I'm Yours*, 2010. New York City, USA. Photo © Luke Jerram

p.24 (1&6). *Play Me, I'm Yours*, 2009. São Paulo, Brazil. Photos © Luke Jerram

p.24 (2). *Play Me, I'm Yours*, 2015. Hong Kong. Photo © PMQ

p.24 (3). *Play Me, I'm Yours*, 2009. Sydney, Australia. Photo © Luke Jerram

p.24 (4). *Play Me, I'm Yours*, 2010. Pécs, Hungary. Photo © Luke Jerram

p.24 (5). *Play Me, I'm Yours*, 2009. London, UK. Photo © Luke Jerram

p.25 (1). *Play Me, I'm Yours*, 2009. Bristol, UK. Photo © Luke Jerram

p.25 (2&5). *Play Me, I'm Yours*, 2008. São Paulo, Brazil. Photos © Luke Jerram

p.25 (3). *Play Me, I'm Yours*, 2010. Barcelona, Spain. Photo © Luke Jerram

p.25 (4). *Play Me, I'm Yours*, 2010. Pécs, Hungary. Photo © Luke Jerram

p.25 (6–7). *Play Me, I'm Yours*, 2010. New York City, USA. Photos © Luke Jerram

pp.26–8. *Park and Slide*, 2014. Bristol, UK. Photo © Luke Jerram

p.28 (top right). *Park and Slide*, 2014. Bristol, UK. Photo © Bristol City Council

pp.28 (bottom) and 29. *Park and Slide*, 2014. Bristol, UK. Photo © Matt Cardy/ Getty Images

p.30. *Lullaby*, 2014. Tilburg, Netherlands. Photos © Luke Jerram

p.31. *Lullaby*, 2015. Derry-Londonderry, Northern Ireland. Photo © Gavan Connolly

p.32 (left). *Withdrawn*, 2015. Bristol, UK. Photo © Luke Jerram

p.32 (right). *Withdrawn*, 2015. Bristol, UK. Photo © Jamie Brightmore

p.33. *Withdrawn*, 2015. Performance by Exultate Singers. Bristol, UK. Photo © Luke Jerram

p.34 (top). *Withdrawn*, 2015. Bristol, UK. Photo © Mark Letheren

p.34. *Withdrawn*, 2015. Bristol, UK. Photos © Luke Jerram

p.34 (bottom). *Withdrawn*, 2015. Bristol, UK. Photo © Paul Box

p.35. *Withdrawn*, 2015. Bristol, UK. Photo © Luke Jerram

pp.36–7. *Withdrawn*, 2015. Bristol, UK. Photo © Paul Box

p.39. *Museum of the Moon*, 2017. *White Night*, Riga, Latvia. Photo © Robert Sils

p.40. *Museum of the Moon*, 2018. *Wye Valley River Festival*, Tintern Abbey, UK. Photo © Gemma Katewood

p.41. *Museum of the Moon*, 2018. *British Science Week*, Leicester Cathedral, UK. Photo © Luke Jerram

p.42. *Museum of the Moon*, 2017. *TEC ART*, Rotterdam, Netherlands. Photo © Luke Jerram

p.43. *Museum of the Moon*, 2017. *Les Tombées de la Nuit*, Rennes, France. Photo © Luke Jerram

p.43. *Museum of the Moon*, 2017. *Festival of Imagineers*, Coventry, UK. Photos © Luke Jerram

p.44. *Museum of the Moon*, 2017. *Light Night*, Leeds, UK. Photo © Carl Milner

p.44. *Museum of the Moon*, 2017. *Cork Midsummer Festival*, Ireland. Photo © Luke Jerram

p.45. *Museum of the Moon*, 2017. University of Bristol, UK. Photo © Neil James

pp.46–7. *Gaia*, 2018. *Bluedot Festival*, Jodrell Bank, UK. Photos © Luke Jerram

p.48. *Gaia*, 2018. Natural History Museum, London, UK. Photos © Luke Jerram

p.49. *Gaia*, 2019. *Hsinchu New Year Festival*, Taiwan. Photo © UrbanArt Studio

pp.50–51. *Mother and Child*, 2018 from *Impossible Garden*, University of Bristol, UK. Photos © Luke Jerram

p.53. *Tide*, 2001. Photo © Luke Jerram

p.54. *Aeolus* sketch by Luke Jerram, 2010

p.54. *Aeolus*, 2011, Lyme Park, Cheshire, UK. Photo © Luke Jerram

p.55. *Aeolus*, 2011. Lyme Park, UK. Photo
© Richard Deane

pp.56–7. *Aeolus*, 2011. Eden Project, UK.
Photos © Luke Jerram

pp.58–9. *Kinetic Chandelier*, 2012. Bristol
and Bath Science Park, UK. Photos
© Luke Jerram

p.60. *HIV*, 2004. Photo © Wellcome
Collection

p.60. Making of *HIV*, 2004. Photo
© Luke Jerram

p.61. *Malaria* (with and without spikes),
2010. Photo © Luke Jerram

p.62. *Papillomavirus, Untitled Future
Mutation* and *HIV*, 2011. Photo
© Luke Jerram

p.62. *E. coli*, 2010. Photo © Luke Jerram

p.63. *Smallpox*, 2008. Photo © Luke Jerram

pp.64–5. *T4 Bacteriophage*, 2011. Photos
© Luke Jerram

pp.66–7. *E. coli*, 2015. *KrebsFest*, The
University of Sheffield, UK. Photos
© Luke Jerram

p.68. *Tōhoku Japanese Earthquake*, 2011.
Photo © Luke Jerram

p.68. Nine-minute seismogram of the
Tōhoku earthquake, 2011.

p.69. Ten seconds of the sound wave
from *Etude No.2* by Philip Glass

p.69. *Apollo*, 2018. Photo © SWNS

pp.70–1. *Maya*, 2013. Bristol Temple
Meads, UK. Photo © Hide the Shark

p.70. Constructing *Maya*, 2013. Photo
© Luke Jerram

p.72. *Han River Pavilion*, 2018. Seoul,
South Korea. Photo © Luke Jerram

p.74. *Treasured City*, 2017 (sixteenth-century
Ivory Fisherwoman; North Lincolnshire
Museum). Photo © Henry Lowther

p.75. *Treasured City*, 2017 (five 18-carat
gold cast objects). Photo © Luke Jerram

pp.76–77. *Treasured City*, 2017 (paintings
exhibited at 20–21 Visual Arts Centre).
Scunthorpe, UK. Photos © Luke Jerram

p.78. *Harrison's Garden* (detail), 2019. The
Ropewalk, Barton-upon-Humber, UK.
Photo © Luke Jerram

p.79. *Harrison's Garden*, 2018. Penrhyn
Castle, UK. Photo © National Trust/
Iolo Penri

pp.80–1. *Just Sometimes*, 2010. *Witte de
With Festival*, Rotterdam, Netherlands.
Photo © Luke Jerram

p.82. *Euclid*, 2015. Photo © Max McClure

p.83. *Euclid* (detail), 2015. Photo
© Luke Jerram

p.84. *Tribute* (detail), 2017. Photo
© Luke Jerram

p.84. CAD mock-up of *Tribute* by
Vicky Leach, 2016

p.85. *Tribute*, 2017. Photo © Luke Jerram

pp.86–87. *Ocean Pavilion*, 2017. Singapore.
Photos © Luke Jerram

p.88. *Han River Pavilion*, 2018. Seoul,
South Korea. Photos © Luke Jerram

pp.89–91. *Han River Pavilion*, 2018. Seoul,
South Korea. Photos © Hangang Art
Park

p.92. *Ghost Plane*, 2004. Photo
© Luke Jerram

p.92. *Dream Director*, 2007. Bristol, UK.
Photo © Luke Jerram

p.92. *Falling Man*, 2008. Photo
© Luke Jerram

p.93. *Portrait Projecting Ring*, 2008.
Photo © Luke Jerram

p.93. *Inhale*, 2018. Photo © Luke Jerram

p.96. *Sky Walk* sketch by Luke Jerram

Back flap: Luke Jerram portrait (*Withdrawn*,
2015). Bristol, UK. Photo © Paul Box

Back cover: *Glass Microbiology: Swine Flu*,
2010. Photo © Luke Jerram

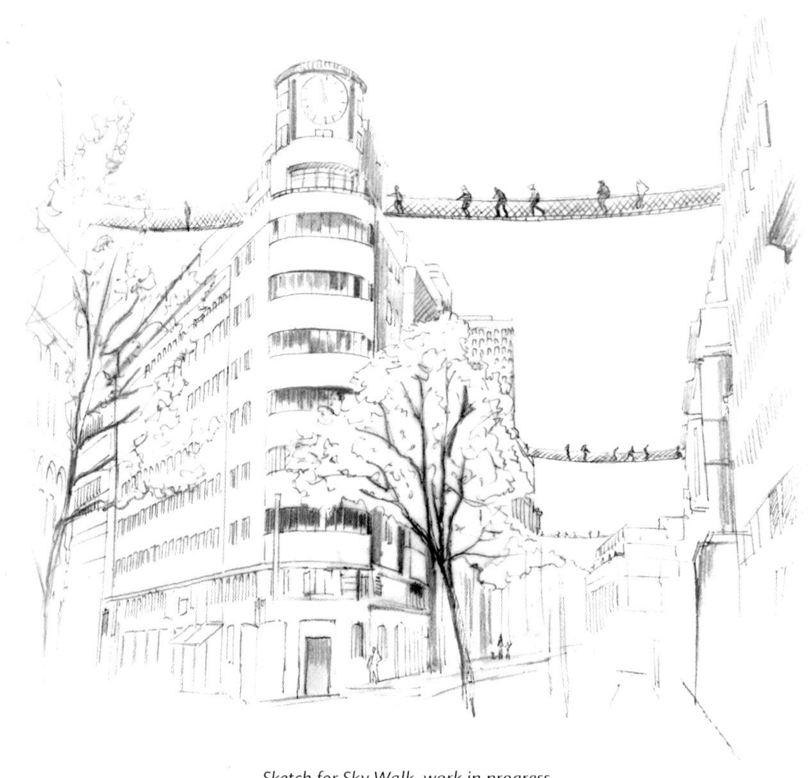

Sketch for Sky Walk, work in progress